⊸ IF ⊸

HEMINGWAY

WROTE

JAVASCRIPT

Angus Croll

Illustrations by Miran Lipovača

NO STARCH PRESS

IF HEMINGWAY WROTE JAVASCRIPT. Copyright © 2015 by Angus Croll.

Printed in Canada
First printing

18 17 16 15 14   1 2 3 4 5 6 7 8 9

ISBN-10: 1-59327-585-4
ISBN-13: 978-1-59327-585-3

Publisher: William Pollock
Production Editor: Alison Law
Cover and Interior Illustrations: Miran Lipovača
Cover Design: Beth Middleworth
Interior Design: Ryan Byarlay and Beth Middleworth
Developmental Editor: Seph Kramer
Copyeditor: Rachel Monaghan
Compositor: Alison Law
Proofreader: Emelie Burnette

For information on distribution, translations, or bulk sales, please contact No Starch Press, Inc. directly:
No Starch Press, Inc.
245 8th Street, San Francisco, CA 94103
phone: 415.863.9900; info@nostarch.com;
www.nostarch.com

Library of Congress Cataloging-in-Publication Data
Croll, Angus.
If Hemingway Wrote JavaScript / by Angus Croll.
      pages cm
ISBN 978-1-59327-585-3 — ISBN 1-59327-585-4
I. Title.
PS3603.R64I38 2014
811'.6—dc23   2014031873

This is a work of parody. It imitates various authors' voices and styles for comic effect.

To Lucy,
George, and
Rosie

Acknowledgments

Thank you to Miran Lipovača for his amazing artwork, which has added so much to this book, and to Jacob Thornton, who, two years ago, invited me to write the original blog post on which this book is based.

Thanks to Andrea Pitzer, author of *The Secret History of Vladimir Nabokov* (Pegasus Books, 2013), for reviewing the Nabokov section; Chris Kubica, editor of *Letters to J.D. Salinger*, (University of Wisconsin Press, 2002), for reviewing the Salinger section; and Joel Turnbull for reviewing the Joyce section. Thanks also to Lucy Kaminska and Graeme Roberts for their contributions. David Foster Wallace's prime number solution was inspired by a solution by Mohammad Shahrizal Prabowo ("JavaScript Sieve Of Atkin.js," *https://gist.github.com/rizalp/5508670*).

Thanks to Bill Pollock at No Starch Press for being persuaded to take on this project against his better judgment, and to Alison Law, Seph Kramer, and everyone else at No Starch for their sterling work and for putting up with my stubbornness.

And a special thanks to the 28 authors, poets, and playwrights who feature in this book, and to Brendan Eich for inventing JavaScript.

CONTENTS

FOREWORD

Angus and I came together over a shared fascination with the outside—the outside being any art, literature, or other expression that runs counter to Silicon Valley.

Around 2012, this coalesced into ##ABC, an IRC book club that never actually read anything. Instead, we were something like a support group, gathering to make sense of our work, what we were doing, and how we were doing it, within the world and through the lens of art and literature.

Some of these conversations later informed writings on *http://byfat.xxx*—posts like Divya Manian's excellent "YES PlZ LETS BURNNNN" or my "rien ne tient en place." But none was quite so well received as Angus's "If Hemingway Wrote JavaScript."

Angus managed to perfectly articulate an issue central to many of us: our antipathy toward "The Good Parts" and the general rhetoric of "the best way." And he did so by celebrating JavaScript's voice and variety, through exploration and experimentation. He was making the language ours, and it was precisely this ownership that served to liberate its potential for expression—its voice making our work not only bearable, but actually exciting.

I wrote, not long after that, "Like an artist painting a bowl of fruit, if I had to express each work the same way—with the only variety being in the fruits themselves—I'd surely have gone mad by now." This insight on writing code, and my career at large, I owe very much to my dear friend Angus and his reflection on creativity and language as craft. It's been fun to watch this idea evolve from IRC to the conference circuit, and now to book form—the medium that inspired this whole line of thought.

Jacob Thornton (@fat)
August 2014

INTRODUCTION

Did Ernest Hemingway write JavaScript? Would Jane Austen have grappled with function hoisting? Was Franz Kafka driven to despair by prototypal inheritance? Brushing aside a few bothersome facts (such as JavaScript not being invented until 1995), it's easy to see why this most literary of computer languages would have piqued the interest of these and other authors.

JavaScript has plenty in common with natural language. It is at its most expressive when combining simple idioms in original ways; its syntax, which is limited yet flexible, promotes innovation without compromising readability. And, like natural language, it's ready to write. Some of JavaScript's more baroque cousins must be edited with an IDE (integrated development environment—a sort of Rube Goldberg machine for coding). JavaScript needs nothing more than a text file and an open mind.

Natural language has no dominant paradigm, and neither does JavaScript. Developers can select from a grab bag of approaches—procedural, functional, and object-oriented—and blend them as appropriate. Most ideas can be expressed in multiple ways, and many JavaScript programmers can be identified by their distinct coding style.

Some of the solutions in this book are, to say the least, unusual. The greatest novelists, poets, and playwrights are those who are prepared to stake out new ground and lay the tracks for those who follow.

"All the best writers . . . have been amongst the flagrant flouters."
—STEVEN PINKER ON PRESCRIPTIVE LANGUAGE[1]

Similarly, the future of the JavaScript language depends on the willingness of its developers to push the limits, to experiment with new patterns that benefit the community at large. When good programmers break a rule, they do it to overcome an arbitrary convention that's hampering their ability to express themselves. Patterns that were once viewed as dangerous and radical—immediately invoked function expressions, callbacks, and modules—are now, thanks to those risk takers, part of the JavaScript mainstream.

Doctrine and dogma are the enemies of good JavaScript. Beware the overly protective mentor; reject the dry and narrow confines of computer science classes. Some developers thrive on rules and constraint, which is why there is Java. If 25 famous authors wrote Java, the result would be more or less the same every time. But JavaScript is much less prescriptive and appeals to those who value creativity over predictability. The best authors and the best JavaScript developers are those who obsess about language, who explore and play with it every day and in doing so develop their own idioms and their own voice.

There is no exquisite beauty without some strangeness in the proportion. —FRANCIS BACON[2]

This book doubles as a survey of known JavaScript idioms. Much of the code explores JavaScript's wilder shores, and while I don't necessarily recommend reproducing the more outlandish examples in your production code, I hope they will help you to think more deeply about the language, and inspire you to write JavaScript that is both expressive and elegant.

Finally, a word about the role of the humanities in software development. As vocational skills have become the order of the day, the liberal arts and social sciences are often dismissed as a sideshow for mushy technophobes or, worse, academics. One victim of this cultural hegemony is diversity (of people, and of approach) in the technology industry. Such narrow focus is self-defeating. Students of the humanities are more likely to have an inductive, open-ended approach to reasoning; they're more likely to probe beyond the standard methodologies; and they're more likely to question accepted practices. By bridging the disciplines, this book will play a small part, I hope, in enriching the gene pool of software development.

The ASSIG

Recently I had a dream in which I assigned homework to Ernest Hemingway and 24 other literary luminaries. Each author received one of five tasks—common coding problems, mostly mathematical—they were to solve using JavaScript.

To my astonishment, after a few days, completed assignments started arriving in my mailbox. Still more remarkable, with the exception of Kafka's accursed effort, they all seemed to work.

Naturally, this was all too good to keep to myself, so I've reproduced their solutions

NMENTS

in this book. To help put the answers in context, I've written a short biography of each author and a brief explanation of what I think they were up to in their code. As a respite between assignments, I've included some poetic interludes: long-forgotten odes documenting their author's struggle with everyone's favorite programming language.

Enjoy!

FIBON

THE ASSIGNMENT:
WRITE A FUNCTION THAT
RETURNS THE FIRST *n*
NUMBERS OF THE FIBONACCI
SEQUENCE.

The Fibonacci sequence is the series of numbers whereby each new number is the sum of the previous two. By convention, the first two numbers of the series are 0 and 1. These are the first 15 Fibonacci numbers:

0, 1, 1, 2, 3, 5, 8, 13, 21, 34, 55, 89, 144, 233, 377

NACCI

1. Ernest Hemingway
2. William Shakespeare
3. André Breton
4. Roberto Bolaño
5. Dan Brown

The sequence is named for Leonardo Pisano (also known as—wait for it—*Fibonacci*), but in a more just world, it would be named the *Pingala* sequence, after the Sanskrit grammarian who documented it a thousand years earlier.

As we progress through the series, the ratio between successive numbers tends toward a constant (roughly 1.61803) known as the *golden ratio*. Some mathematically inclined flora arrange their branches or petals according to the golden ratio—though its prevalence in nature is sometimes overstated.

All my life I've looked at JavaScript as
though I were seeing it for the first time.

ERNEST HEMINGWAY

1899–1961

Ernest Hemingway's work is characterized by direct, uncomplicated prose and a lack of artifice. In his fiction, he describes only the tangible truths: dialog, action, superficial traits. He does not attempt to explain emotion; he leaves it alone. This is not because Hemingway doesn't want his stories to convey feeling—quite the opposite: his intent is to create a vacuum so that it might be filled by the reader's own experience. After all, emotion is more easily felt than described with words:

> *I have tried to eliminate everything unnecessary to conveying experience to the reader so that after he or she has read something it will become a part of his or her experience and seem actually to have happened.* [1]

Hemingway's prose is never showy, and his syntax is almost obsessively conventional. The short, unchallenging sentences and absence of difficult words add a childlike quality to his cadence. He assumes the role of naive observer, all the better to draw his readers into the emotional chaos beneath.

```
1   function fibonacci(size) {
2
3     var first = 0, second = 1, next, count = 2, result = [first, second];
4
5     if (size < 2)
6       return "the request was made but it was not good"
7
8     while (count++ < size) {
9       next = first + second;
10      first  = second;
11      second = next;
12      result.push(next);
13    }
14
15    return result;
16  }
```

The Hemingway paradox is, to some extent, the JavaScript paradox. Just as Hemingway uses only the sparest prose to allow the intricacies of the human condition to surface, JavaScript's terse and direct syntax, when used well, can crystallize complex logic into something tangible and immediate.

Hemingway's Fibonacci solution is code reduced to its essentials, with no word or variable wasted. It's not fancy—maybe it's even a little pedantic—but that's the beauty of Hemingway's writing. There's no need for elaborate logic or showy variable names. Hemingway's JavaScript is plain and clear, and it does only what is necessary—and then it gets out of the way to allow the full glory of the Fibonacci sequence to shine through.

Hemingway didn't suffer fools gladly, so if you ask for a series with fewer than two numbers, he'll just ignore you or complain, "I'm tired and this question is idiotic."

So foul and fair a language I have not seen.

WILLIAM
SHAKESPEARE

1564–1616

In stark contrast to Hemingway's hands-off approach, William Shakespeare probes the human psyche to the fullest. In wondrously expressive verse, he maps the dark crevices of his protagonists and lays bare their souls. Shakespeare's commentary is universal because he recognizes in his subjects those archetypal traits that transcend geography and time.

Shakespeare's plays and sonnets make heavy use of *iambic pentameter,* which was the popular lyrical form of his time. A *foot* is a metrical unit consisting of a stressed syllable and one or more unstressed syllables, and an *iamb* is a two-syllable foot with the second syllable stressed (for example, "reVIEW" or "the CAT"). An iambic pentameter is 5 iambs in a row—10 syllables with stresses on the even-numbered syllables.

Here's a simple couplet in iambic pentameter taken from Shakespeare's "Sonnet 18." Stressed syllables are capitalized:

So LONG as MEN can BREATHE or EYES can SEE,
So LONG lives THIS, and THIS gives LIFE to THEE.

Shakespeare often adds dramatic emphasis by deviating from strict iambic pentameter—he might add an extra syllable or use an alternate stress. In the famous opening line of *Richard III*, the stress of the first foot is reversed (a *trochee*), highlighting the urgency of "now."

NOW is the WINter OF our DISconTENT

```
1   function theSeriesOfFIBONACCI(theSize) {
2
3     //a CALCKULATION in two acts
4     //employ'ng the humourous logick of JAVA-SCRIPTE
5
6     //Dramatis Personae
7     var theResult; //an ARRAY to contain THE NUMBERS
8     var theCounter; //a NUMBER, serv'nt to the FOR LOOP
9
10    //ACT I: in which a ZERO is added for INITIATION
11
12    //[ENTER: theResult]
13
14    //Upon the noble list bestow a zero
15    var theResult = [0];
16
17    //ACT II: a LOOP in which the final TWO NUMBERS are QUEREED and SUMM'D
18
19    //[ENTER: theCounter]
20
21    //Commence at one and venture o'er the numbers
22    for (theCounter = 1; theCounter < theSize; theCounter++) {
23      //By divination set adjoining members
24      theResult[theCounter] = (theResult[theCounter-1] || 1) +
25        theResult[Math.max(0, theCounter-2)];
26    }
27
28    //'Tis done, and here's the answer
29    return theResult;
30
31    //[Exeunt]
32  }
```

Shakespeare's solution comes in the form of a two-act comedy that draws heavily on JavaScript's unusual mannerisms for levity. We're introduced to the cast of players before settling in for the main event. In keeping with the traditions of Elizabethan comedy, the unsettling opening act (in which an incomplete result is prematurely presented) is happily resolved by the final act, affording us much comfort and cheer.

The Bard gets a little wordy, but we wouldn't have it any other way. Several clever devices are employed—for example, the use of `Math.max` ensures that `theResult` does not suffer the indignity of being addressed by a negative index.

Notice that although Shakespeare's comments are in iambic pentameter, he's using weak endings (that is, adding an extra unstressed syllable). Shakespeare frequently used weak endings to denote enquiry or uncertainty (the Elizabethan equivalent of upspeak). We can only assume he found JavaScript as vexing as the rest of us do.

The man who can't visualize a horse galloping
on a tomato is an idiot.

ANDRÉ BRETON

1896–1966

As a founding member of the surrealist movement, André Breton believed dreams were more interesting than reality and should form the basis of our creative endeavors. Nouns are chosen accordingly.

Although it's easy to poke fun at Breton's eccentric metaphors, his work has aged well and is invariably heartfelt and beautiful—the dictation of the unconscious, tenderly transcribed. Here's an excerpt from his gorgeous poem "Facteur Cheval," translated by David Gascoyne.

You remembered then you got up you got out of the train
Without glancing at the locomotive attacked by immense barometric roots
Complaining about its murdered boilers in the virgin forest
Its funnels smoking jacinths and moulting blue snakes
Then we went on, plants subject to metamorphosis
Each night making signs that man may understand
While his house collapses and he stands amazed before the singular packing-cases
Sought after by his bed with the corridor and the staircase [1]

```
1   function Colette(umbrella) {
2     var staircase = 0, galleons = 0, brigantines = 1;
3     var armada = [galleons, brigantines], bassoon;
4     Array.prototype.embrace = [].push;
5
6     while (2 + staircase++ < umbrella) {
7       bassoon = galleons + brigantines;
8       armada.embrace(brigantines = (galleons = brigantines, bassoon));
9     }
10
11    return armada;
12  }
```

Breton has most likely named his Fibonacci exercise after an old flame. He visualizes iteration as a remote staircase plied by a ghostly fleet of ancient vessels. The staircase is of indeterminate length, but an umbrella appears to mark the point beyond which further ascent is impossible. As our protagonist climbs each step, the galleons and brigantines shuffle to the haunting melody of a lone bassoon.

Breton's solution is underpinned by characteristically elegant logic—he's using a comma operator as an ethereal device with which to simultaneously assign `brigantines` to `galleons` and `bassoons` to `brigantines`.

Hats off, André!

We dreamed of JavaScript and woke up screaming.

ROBERTO BOLAÑO

◆▪▮◆━ ● ━◆▮▪◆

1953–2003

If you don't read at least one book by Bolaño before you die, then you've wasted your life.

As the last great Latin American writer of the 20th century, Bolaño is a worthy successor to the magical realists that preceded him, but his writing is harder to characterize. Yes, there are recurring themes: the protagonist (more often than not, an alter ego of the author) as literary action hero, poetry as a beacon of virility or a catalyst for intellectual gang warfare. But for all his professed love of form, Bolaño's work is often messy, sprawling, and inconsistent, liable to lurch into pages of tangential minutiae or take a sudden turn that orphans erstwhile heroes and leaves tantalizing plotlines unresolved. Then again, that might just be the key to his greatness.

Bolaño, a poet by inclination and a novelist by necessity, feels no need to comply with novelistic conventions (as one of his characters puts it, "Rules about plot only apply to novels that are copies of other novels").[1] While more-mainstream authors constantly nudge their characters to a tidy—or at least conclusive—result, Bolaño is content to let his protagonists' fickle psychologies wag the dog. This lack of orchestration makes the random moments of beauty and pain all the more compelling, as demonstrated by this brief paragraph from *The Savage Detectives*:

> *She was looking at me too, and I think I blushed a little. I felt happy. Then right away I ruined it.*[2]

Most of Bolaño's characters are displaced, lost, or desperate. No aspect of human frailty is off-limits. Yet the narrative is rarely dark. On the contrary, Bolaño, as the disinterested observer, exudes naive charm without hubris or homily. When ennui and insecurity once again derail the best laid plans, Bolaño is laughing with us, not at us.

```
1    function LeonardoPisanoBigollo(l) {
2
3      if (l < 0) {
4        return "I'd prefer not to respond. (Although several replies occur to me.)"
5      }
6
7      /**/
8
9      //Everything is getting complicated.
10     for (var i=2,r=[0,1].slice(0,l);i<l;r.push(r[i-1]+r[i-2]),i++)
11
12     /**/
13
14     //Here are some other mathematicians. Mostly it's just nonsense.
15
16     rationalTheorists = ["Archimedes of Syracuse", "Pierre de Fermat (such
       margins, boys!)", "Srinivasa Ramanujan", "René Descartes", "Leonhard
       Euler", "Carl Gauss", "Johann Bernoulli", "Jacob Bernoulli", "Aryabhata",
       "Brahmagupta", "Bhāskara II", "Nilakantha Somayaji", "Omar Khayyám",
       "Muḥammad ibn Mūsā al-Khwārizmī", "Bernhard Riemann", "Gottfried Leibniz",
       "Andrey Kolmogorov", "Euclid of Alexandria", "Jules Henri Poincaré",
       "Srinivasa Ramanujan", "Alexander Grothendieck (who could forget?)", "David
       Hilbert", "Alan Turing", " John von Neumann", "Kurt Gödel", "Joseph-Louis
       Lagrange", "Georg Cantor", "William Rowan Hamilton", "Carl Jacobi", "Évariste
       Galois", "Nikolai Lobachevsky", "Joseph Fourier", "Pierre-Simon Laplace",
       "Alonzo Church", "Nikolai Bogolyubov"]
17
18     /**/
19
20     //I didn't understand any of this, but here it is anyway.
21     return r
22
23     /**/
24
25     //Nothing happens here and if it does I'd rather not talk about it.
26   }
```

True to form, Bolaño's exam paper is peppered with admissions of insecurity, embarrassment, and ignorance. The solution, though rather brilliant, is presented as something of an afterthought. Always obsessive, always tangential, he's much happier offering us a mildly interesting but ultimately useless list of mathematical genii.

The array is named `rationalTheorists` in homage to the *visceral realists*, a gang of guerilla poets featured in *The Savage Detectives*. That group is in turn based on Bolaño's earlier real-life literary gang of two, the *infrarealists*. The `such margins, boys!` comment after the Pierre de Fermat entry is ostensibly a reference to Fermat's famous marginal note, in which he proclaimed he had a proof for his "last theorem" but not enough space to document it. However, it may also be an oblique reference to Ulises Lima, the co-hero of *The Savage Detectives*, who was notorious for scribbling poems in the margins of printed books.

There are other Bolaño traits here: the juxtaposition of long and short paragraphs, the absence of semicolons (mirroring the absence of quotation marks in his novels), and the use of implicit globals (suggesting that each variable is destined to make further appearances in subsequent chapters or even future spin-off novels).

My mind tells me I will never understand JavaScript.
And my heart tells me I am not meant to.

DAN
BROWN

1964–

Dan Brown's big break came in 2003 with *The Da Vinci Code*, a fast-moving, conspiracy-laden murder mystery, in which Brown puts tweed-clad hero Robert Langdon on the trail of the Holy Grail, using Leonardo da Vinci's cryptic brush-work for clues. The initial reception was rhap-sodic. The *New York Times* recommended it with "extreme enthusiasm," describing Brown's writing as "gleefully erudite,"[1] and the public reaction was just as fervent. *The Da Vinci Code* moved quickly into the all-time best-seller list.

Yet the critical acclaim unraveled almost as quickly as Robert Langdon untangled those knotty riddles. By the time the film version was released, the backlash was in full effect. This time, the *New York Times* savagely ridiculed Brown's "um, prose style,"[2] while the *New Yorker* called it "unmitigated junk."[3] Each of Brown's subsequent offerings, including the Dante-inspired *Inferno*, has been a commercial hit—and a critical flop.

Why did Brown's literary reputation collapse? Well, for one, doubts were cast on the accuracy of *The Da Vinci Code*'s historical assertions, and for another, Brown was subject to several lawsuits for plagiarism. But mostly it's about the writing. The cliff-hangers, secret societies, and ancient ciphers may have been enough to distract early reviewers, but sooner or later the shortcomings of Brown's prose needed to be addressed.

Brown's phrasing is excessively weighty, as exemplified by the opening line of *The Da Vinci Code*:

> *Renowned curator Jacques Saunière staggered through the vaulted archway of the museum's Grand Gallery.*[4]

Hanging the staggerer's occupation in front of his name knocks the meter out of balance. Worse, as Geoffrey K. Pullum notes, the information is gratuitous.[5] In the very next paragraph (and a further 10 times in the first two pages), Brown reminds us of Saunière's profession, and since the prologue is entitled "Louvre Museum, Paris, 10:46 pm," it's a safe bet Saunière is renowned. Good fiction, unlike journalism, works the reader's imagination, yet Brown goes to great lengths to spoon-feed the most glaringly obvious detail. He'll often use the same adverb or adjective multiple times on a page, or even within the same paragraph. In the prologue to *The Da Vinci Code* almost every action happens "slowly"; in *Inferno*, we're told no less than four times that Langdon's doctor has "bushy eyebrows."

Another questionable habit of Brown's is his name-dropping of high-end products. As noted by Tom Chivers in the *Telegraph*, Brown rarely misses a chance to shoehorn, QVC-like, their details into the tightest of action sequences ("Yanking his Manurhin MR-93 revolver from his shoulder holster, the captain dashed out of the office," or "Only those with a keen eye would notice his 14-karat gold bishop's ring with purple amethyst, large diamonds, and hand-tooled mitre-crozier appliqué").[6]

But in the end, it doesn't matter. Brown's got a recipe that sells more copies than good writing ever could: take a mysterious organization or artifact (preferably medieval, definitely controversial), gussy it up and dumb it down until it's palatable for the layperson, throw in a generous dash of conspiracy theory and plenty of codes, and serve without editing.

```
1   /*
2   FACT: Some time in 1557, Michelangelo Moribundi, the renowned, bald-headed
    alchemist, fashioned a secret code out of bits of asparagus and placed it in a
    long-forgotten vault ...
3   */
4   function theDaFibonacciCode(numeratiFettucini) {
5     // Wide awake, the bleary-eyed Langdon watched as two tall, lissome number
6     // ones, with big feet and a type of hat, sidled up to the rounded zero ...
7     var ilInumerati = [0,1,1];
8     // while theIntegerThatIncrementsOneByOne morphed eerily into a ... three.
9     theIntegerThatIncrementsOneByOne = 3,
10    // Now the silent ratio that could not be uttered had come to make it right.
11    TheBotticelliVector = 1.61803;
12
13    while (theIntegerThatIncrementsOneByOne < numeratiFettucini) {
14      // Somehow another number one appeared and theIntegerThatIncrementsOneByOne
15      // snatched at it gracefully.
16      theIntegerThatIncrementsOneByOne = theIntegerThatIncrementsOneByOne + 1;
17
18      // The renowned, rounded 16-bit unsigned integer tentatively succumbed to
19      // the strange force of the vector before pushing itself bodily into the
20      // hands of the weakly typed array.
21      ilInumerati.push(
22        Math.round(ilInumerati[theIntegerThatIncrementsOneByOne - 2] *
23          TheBotticelliVector)
24      );
25    }
26
```

```
27    // "Too many elementi?" reminded the five-foot-eleven, bushy-eyebrowed Italian.
28    // Too many elements?
29    if (ilInumerati.length > numeratiFettucini) {
30      // Intelligently, Langdon, sporting a Harris Tweed jacket (J.Crew, $79.99),
31      // sliced it with his Modell 1961 Ausführung 1994 Swiss Army knife.
32      ilInumerati = ilInumerati.slice(0, numeratiFettucini);
33    }
34
35    // The kaleidoscope of truth had been shaken. Now, in front of them, sat the
36    // numerically sequenced sequenza numerica. Like a gleaming cathedral.
37    return ilInumerati;
38
39  }
```

Dan Brown is right at home with the Fibonacci sequence; indeed, it was cunningly used as a highly secure combination for a safe in *The Da Vinci Code*.

But wait, what's this? It seems Brown has discovered a dark and mysterious multiplier (*The Botticelli Vector*, no less), which he uses to derive the next number from the one before. This arithmetic alchemy is all well and good, but we're left wondering whether he knew he could just add the previous two numbers to make the next one. Anyway, it seems to work, so that's probably all that matters.

Judging by the comments, Brown is approaching this problem as though it were one of his blockbusting potboilers. First there's the obligatory FACT, which assures us that what follows is rooted in historical accuracy. Then there's the army of adjectives (because ambiguity is the devil's tool) and the diligent inclusion of product details even as the action reaches a nail-biting climax.

Skipping gingerly over non sequiturs and logical fallacies, we reach the movingly grandiloquent conclusion. Oh, the glory.

The
VARIABLE

after "The Raven"
by Edgar Allan Poe

Once upon a midnight dreary, while I struggled with JQuery,

Sighing softly, weak and weary, troubled by my daunting chore,

While I grappled with weak mapping, suddenly a function wrapping

formed a closure, gently trapping objects that had gone before.

Ah, distinctly I remember, it was while debugging Ember,

As each separate dying member left its host for evermore.

Eagerly I wished the morrow—vainly I had sought to borrow

(From my bookmarked trail of sorrow), APIs from Underscore.

There I sat engaged in guessing the meaning of each cursed expression,

Endless callbacks in procession; nameless functions, nothing more,

This and more I sat divining, strength and spirit fast declining,

Disclose the value we're assigning! Tell me—tell me, I implore!

FACTO

THE ASSIGNMENT:
WRITE A FUNCTION THAT RETURNS THE FACTORIAL OF THE SUPPLIED ARGUMENT.

For any positive integer n, the factorial of n is the result of multiplying n by all the positive integers of lesser value. So the factorial of 5, which is usually written as 5!, is $5 \times 4 \times 3 \times 2 \times 1$, or 120.

RIAL

Someone clever once decided that 0! is 1, though no one can quite remember why. One explanation is that it keeps this pattern happy:

3! = 4!/4
2! = 3!/3
1! = 2!/2
0! = 1!/1

Based on that premise, –1! would be infinity, which is why mention of negative factorials tends to be accompanied by awkward coughing.

*JavaScript is confessional and pure and
all excited with the life of it.*

JACK KEROUAC

1922–1968

Truman Capote famously said of *On the Road*, "That's not writing, it's typing." Jack Kerouac jokingly claimed, "It was dictated by the Holy Spirit! It doesn't need editing!"[1] The popular image of Kerouac as an impulsive, spontaneous speed-writer unconcerned with plot, shape, form, or even punctuation was partly fueled by Kerouac himself, as in his 1968 *Paris Review* interview: "By not revising what you've already written you simply give the reader the actual workings of your mind during the writing itself: you confess your thoughts about events in your own unchangeable way."[2]

The reality was a little less radical. *On the Road* was meticulously prepared and heavily revised (the New York Public Library houses several drafts). Moreover, although Kerouac claimed to dislike the period and mistrust the comma, he used both liberally. Kerouac reflected that the Beat Generation he supposedly founded was "really just an idea in our minds,"[3] and perhaps his version of spontaneous prose was more often vision than reality.

That said, Kerouac's writing constantly evolved in pursuit of the ideal literary voice, and reached its experimental zenith in *The Subterraneans*, which was written in just three days and featured, as the *New York Times* put it, "an almost schizophrenic disintegration of syntax—the effort to reproduce, by a sort of reflex action, the uninterrupted continuum of experience."[4] *The Subterraneans* is the Kerouac myth made real—disparate spurts of melody wrapped in vast poetic sentences like extended improvised jazz passages:

> *a woman of 25 prophesying the future style of America with short almost crewcut but with curls black snaky hair, snaky walk, pale pale junky anemic face and we say junky when once Dostoevski would have said what? if not ascetic but saintly? but not in the least? but the cold pale booster face of the cold blue girl and wearing a man's white shirt but with the cuffs undone untied at the buttons so I remember her leaning over talking to someone after having been slinked across the floor with flowing propelled shoulders, bending to talk with her hand holding a short butt and the neat little flick she was giving to knock ashes but repeatedly with long long fingernails an inch long and also orient and snake-like*[5]

Much more than just typing, Truman.

```
1   /*...the only numbers for me are the mad ones, take forty-three like a steam
    engine with a talky caboose at the end*/ n = 43, /*and that lanky fellow in
    a cocked fedora*/ r = 1 /*then back to our number, our mad number, mad to
    become one*/ while (n > 1) /*mad to descend*/ n--, /*mad to multiply*/ r = r
    * n /*and at the end, you see the blue center-light pop, and everybody goes
    1.4050061177528801e+51...*/
2   r
```

Programming as we know it is anathema to Kerouac. His "Essentials of Spontaneous Prose" included the directive "never afterthink to 'improve' or defray impressions," so we can assume refactoring is out.[6]

Apparently, Kerouac fashioned this solution while in full-blown "jazz prosody" mode because planning was so alien to his process that even functions are verboten. His solution will return only the factorial of 43. If you want the factorial of another number, you'll need to pull a stimulants-induced all-nighter and rewrite it.

Notice how comments are virtually indistinguishable from code. To Kerouac, it's all the same: one long, rhapsodic outpouring. Incidentally, it looks like he's channeling a passage from *On the Road*, blended with a phrase from his 1968 *Paris Review* interview.

A programmer, especially if she has the misfortune of knowing anything, should conceal it as well as she can.

JANE AUSTEN

1775–1817

With dazzling wit, captivating plotlines, and meticulous observation of the manners of her peers, Jane Austen reclaimed the novel from the syrupy sentimentalists who preceded her. Within her perfectly crafted velveteen passages lurks a bitingly cynical parody of the patriarchal society and the tedium of propriety.

Considering the era in which she wrote, Austen was nothing short of a well-mannered revolutionary. The dominant literary form at the end of the 18th century was the *sentimental novel*, a mostly trashy and unrealistic genre that used sappy pathos to push readers' emotional buttons and an aura of mushy goodness to tug at their heartstrings. Austen's works, while superficially resembling this genre, ridicule the sentimentalist trifecta of fairy-tale love, chivalry, and honor in favor of more pertinent realities: money, wisdom, and prejudice.

Austen also pioneered the use of *free indirect speech*, in which the narrative appears to express sentiments on the protagonist's behalf. In this excerpt from *Emma*, the perspective gradually shifts from objective commentary to personal exclamation so that by the third sentence the point of view (and the attitude) is entirely Emma's:

> *It was a very great relief to Emma to find Harriet as desirous as herself to avoid a meeting. Their intercourse was painful enough by letter. How much worse, had they been obliged to meet!*[1]

By weaving their opinions into the narrative's authoritative mantle, Austen fosters trust and empathy for her characters.

Austen was merciless in her contempt for the social mores of her time and frequently used free indirect speech as an agent of derision. Here are a few stinging one-liners from *Sense and Sensibility*:

> *He was not an ill-disposed young man, unless to be rather cold-hearted, and rather selfish, is to be ill-disposed.*

> *Her manners had all the elegance which her husband's wanted. But they would have been improved by some share of his frankness and warmth.*

> *However dissimilar in temper and outward behavior, they strongly resembled each other in that total want of talent and taste.*

> *Lady Middleton was more agreeable than her mother, only in being more silent.*[2]

Today Austen is as revered as ever, both as an exceptional wit and as a voice against the privilege, bigotry, and artifice that continue to thrive in modern society.

```
1    var factorial = (function() {
2      //She declared the ledger to be very plain. But with the happiest prospects!
3      var ledger = {};
4
5      return function reckoning(quantity) {
6        if (isNaN(quantity)) {
7          console.log("I have not the pleasure of understanding you.");
8          return;
9        }
10       //It is a truth universally acknowledged that two values can only be judged
11       //truly agreeable by means of the treble equal symbol...
12       if (quantity === 0) {
13         return 1;
14       }
15       //Mr Crockford teaches that we should be wary of inherited property...
16       if (ledger.hasOwnProperty(quantity)) {
17         return ledger[quantity];
18       }
19       //No sooner was each function finished than the next one began!
20       return ledger[quantity] = quantity * reckoning(quantity - 1);
21     };
22   })();
```

Jane Austen's solution demonstrates two pleasing characteristics for which she is justly famous. First, there's her attention to plot and structural integrity, reflected here in the neat packaging of her code: She invokes the module pattern, hiding away the historical data (or `ledger`) within the folds of the superstructure. Second is her sometimes playful, sometimes subversive send-up of the powers that be and their ridiculous conventions.

At first glance, Austen's code appears to be submissive, yielding to every overbearing commandment and pious proclamation set forth by the more pedantic leaders in our community. Yet a closer reading reveals that this is nothing less than a full-on parody of the social norms of JavaScript. There are several clues to Austen's real intent: Checking if the argument is a number mocks edge-case mania; overembellished (and often free indirect) comments poke fun at those who insist that `==` is the devil's work; and the satirical fawning over the nice Mr. Crockford is an ironic justification for the all-too-common misuse of the `hasOwnProperty` method.

Austen is on top of her game here, simultaneously gaining approval from the purveyors of code dogma while winking furiously at those who can see beyond the artifice and discern the subtext.

When a man is tired of JavaScript he is tired of life.

SAMUEL JOHNSON

1709–1784

The popular image of Samuel Johnson as a con-
vivial sage with a witty remark for every occasion
owes much to James Boswell's renowned 1791
biography, *Life of Samuel Johnson*. But there's a
darker side to Johnson that Boswell, whether by
reverence or ignorance, tends to underplay.

Johnson experienced ill health for most of
his life. Aside from a series of physical ailments,
there were copious mental gremlins. Johnson was
an obsessive-compulsive, it's likely he suffered
from Tourette syndrome (his attempts at teach-
ing were stymied by constant facial grimaces and
nervous tics, which scared away patrons), and
he was subject to crippling depression. These
numerous maladies, exacerbated by parental
debt, condemned Johnson to financial hardship
for more than 30 years. It was Johnson's sheer
erudite brilliance, combined with an impeccable
work ethic, that belatedly won him the recogni-
tion that would lift him out of poverty.

In 1746, a consortium of prominent book-
sellers commissioned Johnson to compile
A Dictionary of the English Language in two
volumes. Johnson's was not the first English
dictionary, but previous efforts were highly

selective, mainly focusing on uncommon words (which, paradoxically, are usually easier to define), and gave little or no indication of usage. Johnson's dictionary defined 42,000 words, and each definition was supplemented with one or more literary quotations illustrating usage. It's a testament to Boswell's influence that Johnson's dictionary is often viewed as a humorous work; yet, while there are a handful of witty definitions (most famously the self-deprecating explanation of lexicographer as "a harmless drudge"), the dictionary is genuinely scholarly and was still considered the preeminent English dictionary 100 years after it was first published.

Johnson—who was also a biographer, poet and literary critic—was remarkably prolific, but his writing is sometimes criticized for being monotonous, even pedantic; he would often embrace opposing arguments in a single sentence, as though presenting both sides of an internal squabble. Yet therein lies Johnson's attraction. While most writers gloss over their fickleness of opinion to present a unified thesis, Johnson invites us into his conflicted soul to reason along with him. The result is warm and richly human.

```coffeescript
1   # In which various NUMBERS are summon'd by
2   # means of ELECTRONICK CONJURY.
3   factorial = (n) ->
4     # All argument is against it, yet all belief is for it.
5     return 1 unless n
6
7     # Ingenious sophistry to prove the palp'bly OBVIOUS
8     return 1 if n is 1
9
10    # Recursion (n.)
11    # a program that calls 'pon itself in the manner of
12    # a dog returning unto its VOMIT
13    return n * factorial n - 1
```

When I opened Johnson's completed assignment, I found a short note from the good doctor, explaining why he had chosen to use CoffeeScript: "Sir, the funcktion key-word is an ALBATROSS, and the curly brace is worthless FILIGREE. I desire a clean and artickulate script for the dockumenting of my varied MUSINGS."

And indeed Johnson's solution would be lucidly elegant, were it not liberally peppered with grouchy witticisms betraying his characteristic self-doubt and internal second-guessing. He expresses his incredulity that `factorial(0)` is 1, is amused that it should require an entire statement to ascertain that `factorial(1)` is indeed 1, and finishes with a sardonic definition of recursion lifted, presumably, from his own dictionary.

Johnson's solution lies at the intersection of art and parody—a gentle self-mocking blended with uncluttered expression and genuine beauty. A doff of the tricorn to you, sir.

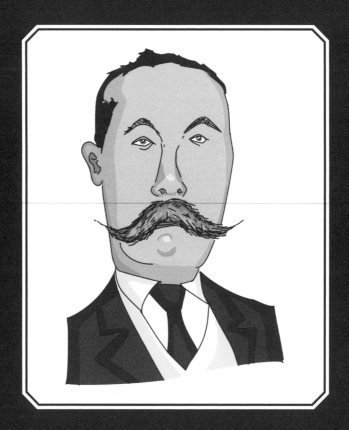

*It is better to learn JavaScript late
than never to learn it at all.*

SIR ARTHUR CONAN DOYLE

1859–1930

Sir Arthur Conan Doyle was a medical doctor by training and a writer by destiny. He wrote scores of short stories, historical novels, romances, and fantasy fiction, as well as countless nonfiction books on topics as diverse as the military, injustice, and spiritualism. But he's best known as the creator of the iconic detective, Sherlock Holmes.

There's nothing groundbreaking about the format of the Holmes stories; the narrative is mostly linear and the prose exhibits plenty of Victorian pomposity. Nor is the character of Holmes entirely original—Doyle all but conceded that he used Edgar Allan Poe's maverick detective C. Auguste Dupin as a blueprint (Doyle also draws heavily on Poe's portrayal of the macabre). But the writing is lively, and we're drawn to the emotional chasm between the brilliant but nutty Holmes and his eminently reasonable but pedestrian sidekick Watson. On top of that, Doyle concocts a delightfully freakish cast of minor characters, evoking London's ghoulish underbelly.

Holmes himself is deeply flawed. He's lazy, conceited, vain, impetuous, and moody. He's a drug addict who distrusts women and shuns relationships, and there's a strong suggestion of autism. A peerless knowledge of poisons and tobacco varieties contrasts with almost total ignorance of basic science. (Shortly after their first meeting, Watson is astonished to learn that Holmes does not understand that the earth revolves around the sun.) Even his methods are questionable. What Holmes claims as deduction is actually induction—a series of guesses based on the study of minutiae:

> *The nocturnal visitors were two in number, one remarkable for his height (as I calculated from the length of his stride), and the other fashionably dressed, to judge from the small and elegant impression left by his boots. . . . Having sniffed the dead man's lips I detected a slightly sour smell, and I came to the conclusion that he had had poison forced upon him.*[1]

Yet, whether by luck or good judgment, he's a winner; he knows it, and so do we.

```javascript
1   "use strict";
2   //In solving a problem of this sort, the grand thing is to reason backwards...
3
4   //Some things are easier known than explained.
5   var caseHistory = new Object({2:2, 6:3});
6
7   function unfactorial(evidence){
8     //It is my belief, Watson, founded upon my experience, that a
9     //mathematician would never chase the factorial of zero.
10    if (evidence === 1) { return 1; }
11
12    //Seek out logical precedence.
13    if (caseHistory[evidence]){
14      //Elementary!
15      return caseHistory[evidence];
16    }
17
18    //Eliminate the impossible.
19    if (evidence === 0 || evidence % 24 !== 0) {
20      return "charlatans!";
21    }
22
23    //At this point deductions may be drawn.
24    var theDeduction, numerator = evidence, denominator = 1;
25    while (numerator % denominator === 0) {
26      numerator = numerator / denominator++;
27      if (numerator === denominator) {
28        theDeduction = numerator;
29      }
30    }
31
32    theDeduction = theDeduction || "impostors";
33
34    //What one man can invent, another can discover.
35    caseHistory[evidence] = theDeduction;
36    //What remains, however improbable, must be the truth.
37    return theDeduction;
38  }
```

Doyle was clearly in full deerstalker- and magnifying glass–mode when solving the case of the hidden factorial.

Or rather, unfactorial. Why? Because Holmes always works backward toward the deed's inception. As he puts it, "It is a capital mistake to theorise before one has data. Insensibly one begins to twist facts to suit theories, instead of theories to suit facts."[2] In this case, the data is the outcome of existing factorial procedures, and from this, Holmes establishes the theory that will track down those fiendish numbers at the operation's source.

As expected, Holmes's process is precise and meticulously ordered; clearly, he was an early adopter of the imperative approach to programming. Notice he also directs his utility to run in strict mode; he'll tolerate no sloppiness. He starts with an educated guess—characteristically disguised as certainty—in assuming that no sane person would seek the factorial of 0. Holmes quickly gains his stride so that by the end of the exercise, he imperiously derides those who would supply false arguments as charlatans and impostors. Case closed, Watson.

Writing in JavaScript is the most ingenious torture ever devised for sins committed in previous lives.

JAMES JOYCE

◆▪—◆▪▸—◆—◂▪◆—▪◆

1882–1941

James Joyce spent most of his adult life abroad, but he always longed for his native Dublin and never wrote about any other place. Joyce's Dublin is a nebulous composite of found objects—places, people, words—reclaimed from his former years. For Joyce, all of humanity was contained within the city of his memory:

> *I always write about Dublin, because if I can get to the heart of Dublin I can get to the heart of all the cities of the world. In the particular is contained the universal.* [1]

Although Joyce's writing is notoriously opaque, nothing is hidden from the persevering reader. There's no deceit, no posture or literary swagger; Joyce's characters ring true, and he observes them with fierce objectivity. The apparent paradox owes much to the unusual narrative approach that characterizes Joyce's later works.

Conventional literature is a clinical device whereby the universe of thoughts and intentions, speech and actions is pruned and honed into a clean, digestible flow, focused on the novelist's chosen themes. Joyce's first published fiction, the short-story collection *Dubliners*, was somewhat bound by this tradition. But by the time he wrote *Ulysses*, Joyce had abandoned narrative authority entirely, in favor of an urgent, in-the-moment stream of consciousness in which both narrator and protagonist relate disjointed scraps of ephemera that mirror the random, cluttered, ever-changing character of interior thought.

Ulysses ends with Molly Bloom's remarkable 45-page monologue. After (perhaps) mishearing her husband, who by now is sleeping in bed beside her, Molly drifts into an immense and meandering thought chain that offers a priceless window into her private reality, a digression that would be considered pointless in a conventional novel.

Here's Molly as she gazes idly at her cat:

> *I wonder do they see anything that we cant staring like that when she sits at the top of the stairs so long and listening as I wait always what a robber too that lovely fresh place I bought I think Ill get a bit of fish tomorrow or today is it Friday yes I will with some blanc-mange with black currant jam like long ago not those 2 lb pots of mixed plum and apple from the London and Newcastle* [2]

Joyce's final novel, *Finnegans Wake*, was 17 years in the making and is an entirely unprecedented (and to many, unintelligible) journey into the psyche of nocturnal Dublin. In an attempt to capture the vocabulary of sleep and dreams, Joyce discarded not only traditional narrative but also the English language itself. Almost every sentence is an otherworldly mélange of invented words, puns, and double meaning.

> *Tugbag is Baggut's, when a crispin sokolist besoops juts kamps or clapperclaws an irvingite offthedocks. A luckchange, I see. Thinking young through the muddleage spread, the moral fat his mental leans on.*[3]

Remarkably, over the years, tenacious readers have pieced together a discernible plotline, though they're still divided over the identity of the characters.

The latter part of Joyce's life was quite miserable. The scorn of his slighted compatriots, together with censorship and the iron rule of the Catholic Church, left him permanently exiled from the Ireland that he loved as much as loathed. He suffered from chronic illness and virtual blindness. Worst of all, perhaps, he felt let down by a public who was at best outraged by, and at worst ambivalent to, his staggering talent and relentless literary ambition.

```
1    function hacktorial(integette) {
2      var nonthings = [undefined, null, false, 0, '']
3      var resultution = 1
4      if(integette == 0) {
5        //behold the strangerous zeroine!
6        resultution = 1;
7      } else {
8        while(integette > 1)
9        //caligulate by multicapables
10       resultution = resultution * integette--
11     }
12
13     with(resultution) {
14       var duodismal =  Function('return this').call(toString(12))
15       var disemvowel = Function("n","return n ? parseInt(n,12) : '0'")
16       return [
17         disemvowel(duodismal.slice(0,-1)),
18         'shillings and',
19         disemvowel(duodismal[duodismal.length-1]), 'pence'
20       ].join(' ')
21     }
22     //klikkaklakkaklasssklopatzkacreppycrottygraddaghsemihsammhappluddyappladdyponko!
23   }
```

Where do we start? Joyce is not content with merely solving the problem at hand; he is compelled to turn it into a raucous adventure on the high seas of verbal heresy.

This solution continues the Joycean tradition of generating amusingly intuitive portmanteaus (featured most abundantly in *Finnegans Wake*). Here's a mini-glossary for the Joyce-less among us:

hacktorial   The function is a hack on factorial.

integette   If you don't use a small integer, it's all ruined.

nonthings   For reasons best known to Joyce, our function begins with a declaration of falsey values.

resultation   The result of the computation.

strangerous   Both strange and dangerous.

zeroine   Our heroine, value 0.

caligulate   To calculate, presumably with a liberal dose of tyranny.

multicapables   Items capable of being multiplied.

duodismal   The bleakness that is the duo-decimal system (i.e., base-12).

disemvowel   To remove all vowels—or in this case, all letters.

Joyce's syntax is typically unorthodox; all focus is on the code. There are no semicolons, he's using rarely seen function constructors, and his solution hinges on the much pilloried, though highly expressive, `with` statement.

By the time he's halfway through, the problem is already solved, but Joyce insists on converting the result into the currency of the time: shillings and pence. As with much of Joyce's work, there's a degree of method to such apparent madness: The factorial of every number over 3 is divisible by 12—which also happens to be the number of pennies in a shilling.

Here's what we get:

```
hacktorial(3) //"0 shillings and 6 pence"
hacktorial(4) //"2 shillings and 0 pence"
hacktorial(7) //"420 shillings and 0 pence"
hacktorial(21) //"4257578514309120000 shillings and 0 pence"
```

Macbeth's

LOST CALLBACK

after a soliloquy from Macbeth
by William Shakespeare

SEYTON

The tests, my lord, have failed.

MACBETH

I should have used a promise;

There would have been an object ready made.

Tomorrow, and tomorrow, and tomorrow,

Loops o'er this petty code in endless mire,

To the last iteration of recorded time;

And all our tests have long since found

Their way to dusty death. Shout, shout, brief handle!

Thine's but a ghoulish shadow, an empty layer

That waits in vain to play upon this stage;

And then is lost, ignored. Yours is a tale

Told by an idiot, full of orphaned logic

Signifying nothing.

HAPPY

THE ASSIGNMENT:
WRITE A FUNCTION THAT DETERMINES IF THE SUPPLIED ARGUMENT IS A HAPPY NUMBER.

Take any positive integer, add the squares of its digits, rinse, and repeat. If you eventually reach 1, the original number is happy; otherwise, it's inconsolable.

NUMBERS

Here are a couple of examples:

19 is happy because

$1^2 + 9^2 = 82$
$8^2 + 2^2 = 68$
$6^2 + 8^2 = 100$
$1^2 + 0^2 + 0^2 = 1$

4 is unhappy because

$4^2 = 16$
$1^2 + 6^2 = 37$
$3^2 + 7^2 = 58$
$5^2 + 8^2 = 89$
$8^2 + 9^2 = 145$
$1^2 + 4^2 + 5^2 = 42$
$4^2 + 2^2 = 20$
$2^2 + 0^2 = 4$

And the cycle repeats indefinitely . . .

*I'm aware that many of my friends will be saddened
and shocked, or shock-saddened by JavaScript.*

J.D.
SALINGER

1919–2010

J.D. Salinger's legacy is a chronicle of shattered illusions. Three horrific years as a combat soldier in World War II left Salinger deeply traumatized. When he returned to America in 1946, he found a society preoccupied with shallow affectation and largely oblivious to the real-world horrors that were now deeply ingrained in his damaged psyche. Considering himself adrift in a world of "phonies," he sought emotional solace in his writing.

Salinger frequently features children whose honesty and vitality stand in sharp contrast to the duplicity and spiritual emptiness of his grown-up characters. In Salinger's short story "A Perfect Day for Bananafish," Seymour, a mentally fragile war veteran (something of a Salinger alter ego), is treated with indifference by his wife and seen as a monster by his mother-in-law. But Sybil, a young girl Seymour meets on the beach, is in awe of the flawed adult, and their relationship is the high point of an otherwise cheerless story.

Salinger's most famous work, the persistently popular (and regularly banned) *The Catcher in the Rye*, is a candid first-person account of 16-year-old Holden Caulfield's perilous transition to adulthood. One reason for *Catcher*'s enduring popularity is that Salinger nails the irrationality and complexity of adolescence. Holden is deeply repelled by the fraudulence of adults yet exhibits plenty of swagger and posturing of his own; he's an insufferable delinquent, yet he's charmingly naive, compassionate, and keenly intelligent. Only Holden could be found earnestly discussing *Romeo and Juliet* with two nuns he encounters in a Grand Central Station sandwich bar, while playing hooky from the boarding school that's already expelled him.

The only time Holden is truly at ease is when he's with his 10-year-old sister, Phoebe, whom he loves unconditionally. Here's Holden giddily watching Phoebe on the carousel as Salinger, once again, drives home the redemptive power of children:

> *I was damn near bawling, I felt so damn happy, if you want to know the truth. I don't know why. It was just that she looked so damn nice, the way she kept going around and around, in her blue coat and all.*[1]

```
1   // Most numbers are goddamn phonies, I swear to God.
2   function howAreYaAnyway(number) {
3     // What I thought I'd do, I thought I'd loop. I mean it.
4     do {
5       if (number < 5) break
6       thisNextNumber = 0
7       // Making it a string. I'm serious.
8       number = String(number)
9       for (i in number)
10        thisNextNumber += number[i]*number[i]
11      // Putting the next one right back in the old one. Corny as hell I'll admit it.
12      number = thisNextNumber
13    } while (true)
14    // Only about five numbers are really happy, that kills me.
15    return "I'm " + ['H','Unh'][number==1?0:1] + "appy, I really am"
16  }
```

Salinger's solution bears all the hallmarks of Holden Caulfield's first-person narrative—Holden's conflicted psyche is on full display. He tells us he has no time for numbers, but can't stop himself from dutifully working through the exercise. He takes copious liberties with syntax and form—he leaves out all of the semicolons and most of the braces; he uses `break` and abuses ternaries, apparently just for kicks—and yet his logic is underpinned by a fierce intellect, not to mention originality. Who else realized that all unhappy numbers end up resolving to 4? To his mind, the conventional practice of laboriously accumulating a record of previously tested numbers to avoid infinite looping is as unnecessary as it is phony.

Holden knows he's clever, yet he's also insecure—almost every comment ends with a self-deprecating swipe at his own logic, just in case he's wrong. His final comment betrays his acute sensitivity toward others, even those he purports to dislike. He starts out by lambasting all numbers as phonies, yet he's still distressed that so few of them are genuinely happy.

I'm not kidding.

Follow your heart, but take JavaScript with you.

TUPAC

SHAKUR

1971–1996

It's hard to reconcile the two identities of Tupac Amaru Shakur. One was cerebral, sensitive, and compassionate: an actor and poet in his early teens, a devotee of Shakespeare who addressed women's struggles, child abuse, and poverty in his lyrics. The other was a violent, gun-toting embodiment of the *gangsta rap* movement: in and out of prison and sporting a "Thug Life" tattoo across his stomach, killed at the age of 25 by an unknown attacker's bullet.

As a child, Tupac was influenced by the Black Power movement (both of his parents were active members of the Black Panther party). He recalled that the term *Black Power* had been "like a lullaby when I was a kid," and his heroes from that movement would have a profound influence on his work: "I just continued where they left off. I tried to add spark to it, I tried to be the new breed, the new generation. I tried to make them proud of me."[1]

Highly inventive and literate, Tupac used his sociopolitical rapping as an outlet for his righteous passion. His first album, *2Pacalypse Now*, was a raw and powerful commentary on the alienation of Black America. Tupac's message was social justice, but his approach was often aggressive:

> *The underground railroad on an uprise*
> *This time the truth's gettin' told, heard enough lies*
> *I told 'em fight back, attack on society*
> *If this is violence, then violent's what I gotta be.*[2]

This menacing stage persona would prove to be his undoing. Growing up, he had learned ballet, acting, and music. In response to a question about his involvement in childhood gangs, Tupac replied, "Shakespeare gangs. I was the Mouse King in *The Nutcracker*. . . . There was no gangs. I was an artist."[3] While he pined for that lost innocence, he had an almost pathological fascination with thug life and gang warfare.

Tupac's 1995 album, *Me Against the World* (released while he was in prison), directly addressed this mental turmoil. It is, as *Rolling Stone* put it, "by and large a work of pain, anger and burning desperation—[it] is the first time 2Pac has taken the conflicting forces tugging at his psyche head-on."[4] Time and again, in his lyrics, Tupac rejects the thug life while acknowledging he is past the point of no return and prophesying his imminent demise:

> *There was no mercy on the streets, I couldn't rest*
> *I'm barely standin', 'bout to go to pieces, screamin' peace*
> *And though my soul was deleted, I couldn't see it*
> *I had my mind full of demons tryin' to break free*[5]

Tupac may lack the lyrical finesse and sophisticated rhyming patterns of more high-craft rappers. Most of his words are short and to the point; he's not trying to be clever. But that raw, unrefined honesty is exactly what packs such a punch. Impulsive and off-guard, Tupac's contrasting emotions—hostility and humility, confidence and doubt, strength and vulnerability—coexist poignantly.

```javascript
1   var theyDigits, theStash, nextFigure, anEmptyHash = {}
2
3   function isChillin(maFigure) {
4     theStash = theStash || anEmptyHash
5     nextFigure = 0 /* picture me nillin' */
6     /* in preparation fo' fillin' */
7     /* they precondition is partition so */ doFissionOn(maFigure)
8     sumTheySquares() /* quadratic addition, like a math'matician  */
9     /* and the stash is the hash caching all my dead figures */
10    /* if your value is one, you won, or if you in tha' stash, you done */
11    if (nextFigure == 1) return "chillin"
12    if (theStash[nextFigure] == 'x') return "illin"
13    theStash[nextFigure] = 'x' /* keepin' the history */
14    /* breakin' the chain of iteration misery */
15    return isChillin(nextFigure) /* recurse, rejigga, re-traverse the verse */
16  }
17
18  function doFissionOn(n) {theyDigits = n.toString().split('')}
19  function sumTheySquares() {theyDigits.forEach(function(n){nextFigure += n*n})}
```

Tupac's solution fuses native JavaScript with his characteristic lyrical devices: internal rhyming, assonance, alliteration, and consonance. It flows and it compiles.

Original and rebellious, Tupac ignores the best practices of the establishment, sneering at semicolons and deriding the use of curly brackets in conditionals. Moreover, he refuses to label numbers as *happy* or *sad*, preferring to cast them as either *chillin* or *illin*. Much to the annoyance of purists, the utility functions (`doFissionOn` and `sumTheySquares`) are referenced long before they are finally defined. (Tupac gets JavaScript, and he knows that function hoisting will take care of them.)

True to form, he employs a variety of attitudes to tell a story of disparate fortunes. While the opening lines are cocky and dripping with swagger, the code takes a darker, more introspective turn as Tupac considers the number's dead colleagues callously boxed up in the stash and wonders if this number will suffer a similar fate. Near the end, he contemplates the pain of those caught in "iteration misery" but manages to restore a more positive vibe by suggesting a remedy ("keepin' the history") and ultimately offering fresh hope in the form of a new verse.

Keep ya head up.

A woman must have money and a room of her own
if she is to write JavaScript.

VIRGINIA WOOLF

1882–1941

Virginia Woolf was a pioneer of lyricism in modern literature. Leaning heavily on stylistic devices—alliteration, assonance, rhythm—Woolf's unhurried language has a lush dreamlike quality. The following passage from *To the Lighthouse* is ostensibly prose, but the meter is so strong and the wordplay so rich that it reads like poetry:

> *The autumn trees, ravaged as they are, take on the flash of tattered flags kindling in the gloom of cool cathedral caves where golden letters on marble pages describe death in battle and how bones bleach and burn far away in Indian sands.*[1]

Her sentences, unfettered by formal structure, are rarely pithy and frequently expand into lengthy streams of consciousness, strung together with semicolons and em dashes.

Considering perception to be the greater part of reality, Woolf presents a composite truth assembled not from words or deeds but from a million private thoughts—in her own words, "a whole made of shivering fragments."[2] Woolf moves between her characters, probing each psyche relentlessly and flooding the page with their unspoken thoughts. In this devastating excerpt from *Mrs. Dalloway*, Clarissa has just learned of a humiliating snub:

> *She put the pad on the hall table. She began to go slowly upstairs, with her hand on the bannisters, as if she had left a party, where now this friend now that had flashed back her face, her voice; had shut the door and gone out and stood alone, a single figure against the appalling night . . . feeling herself suddenly shrivelled, aged, breastless, the grinding, blowing, flowering of the day, out of doors, out of the window, out of her body and brain which now failed.*[3]

Nearly a century later, Woolf's version of reality feels as potent as ever.

```
1   function happy(number) {
2     var next, numeral, noneOfThese = [];
3
4     //unless the number was nothing; or one; or unless it had been already tried
5     while (number && number != 1 && noneOfThese[number] == null) {
6       next = 0, numerals = String(number).split('')
7       //digits forced apart, now multiplied, now cast aside; in service of what?
8       while (next = next+numerals[0]*numerals[0], numerals.shift(), numerals.length);
9       noneOfThese[number] = true, number = next
10    }
11
12    //to be one; alone; happily
13    return number == 1
14  }
```

If the semicolon is the period of JavaScript, then the comma operator is its semicolon. Programmer Woolf loves the comma operator, and in her happy numbers solution, she uses it to excess. The result is a dreamy, melancholic form of JavaScript (is there any other?) made dreamier still by the heavy, almost dangerous level of *n* alliteration and some gorgeously expressive pairings. In *To the Lighthouse*, Woolf writes of night's shadows: "They lengthen; they darken"; in her happy numbers solution we get the wistfully poetic `numerals.shift(), numerals.length`.

The mood is volatile. Woolf begins the exercise confidently enough, yet even as she methodically talks us through the process, doubts emerge. Gradually, her inner voice permeates the commentary; she anxiously relates each number's cold dissection. All this control, this manipulation . . . And to what end?

At the conclusion, Woolf equates the value of happiness (i.e., the number 1) with the joys of solitude, perhaps in reference to her famous essay "A Room of One's Own," in which she makes the case that women writers should be given literal and figurative space.

Ther nis no werkman, whatsoevere he be,
That may code JS both wel and hastily.

GEOFFREY CHAUCER

1343–1400

As one of the first poets to write in the Middle English vernacular, Geoffrey Chaucer made lexical and stylistic choices that had a major influence on the language and literature that followed. Although he almost always wrote in verse, many of Chaucer's works run for hundreds of pages and are considered precursors to the modern prose novel. Chaucer's relaxed style combined irreverent humor with compassion and an understanding of the human condition that was rare for an author of his time.

Chaucer's most famous work, *The Canterbury Tales*, chronicles a diverse assortment of pilgrims as they ride from London to a shrine in Canterbury. The pilgrims (each identified by profession—the Knight, the Miller, the Summoner, the Pardoner, and so on) take turns delivering the narrative, and although they're drawn from every social stratum and both sexes, Chaucer slips effortlessly into each persona. The rich collage of perspectives that emerges provides an invaluable social record of the period. Chaucer leans heavily on the stereotypes of the day, but his portraits are affectionate—never pompous—and the effect is funny, informal, and charming.

Because there is no contemporary recording of Chaucer's verse, nor a continuous tradition of performance, we can't be certain of the intended meter. Even the number of syllables is up for debate; by Chaucer's time, pronunciation of trailing vowels was losing favor in conversational English but persisted in the written form. However, it's generally agreed that Chaucer's long-line verses are to be read as rhyming couplets of iambic pentameter, often called *riding rhyme* in an allusion to the rhythm of the pilgrims' horses in *The Canterbury Tales* (and so perhaps meant to be delivered at a faster clip than, say, Shakespeare's walkable pentameter).

Chaucer's version of Middle English, though unusual to modern English speakers, can be fairly easily inferred (especially with the help of a basic glossary).[1] Here's an excerpt from the "General Prologue" to *The Canterbury Tales*, in which Chaucer apologizes for the bawdy nature of the upcoming text by explaining that he is duty-bound to faithfully reproduce his subjects' accounts:

> *Whoso shal telle a tale after a man,*
> *He moot reherce as ny as evere he kan*
> *Everich a word, if it be in his charge,*
> *Al speke he never so rudeliche or large,*
> *Or ellis he moot telle his tale untrewe,*
> *Or feyne thyng, or fynde wordes newe.*[2]

And here's the same verse in modern English:

> *Who tells the tale of any other man*
> *Should render it as nearly as he can,*
> *If it be in his power, word for word,*
> *Though from him such rude speech was never heard.*
> *If he does not, his tale will be untrue,*
> *The words will be invented, they'll be new.*[3]

```
1   // Bifil that in this seson, on this day,
2   // In Eich-ian riddle solemnly I lay,
3   // To telle yow al the condicioun
4   // Of nombres parfit and oothers gone astray.
5   function isGladNombre(nombre, ungladNombres) {
6     ungladNombres = ungladNombres || [];
7     if (ungladNombres.indexOf(nombre) > -1) {
8       return 'untrewe';
9     } else {
10      return nombre == 1 ||
11        isGladNombre(summonTheSqwares(nombre), ungladNombres.concat(nombre));
12    }
13
14    function summonTheSqwares(nombre) {
15      return ooneFoldeNombres(nombre).map(sqwarer).reduce(summoner);
16    }
17  }
18
19  // Men intente is pleyn, reveeled anon...
20  // For nombres giv'n, retorne the somme.
21  function summoner(nombre, ootherNombre) {
22    return nombre + ootherNombre;
23  }
24
25  // It suffreth me to tell in rhyme
26  // Of acht tymes acht and nyne tymes nyne.
27  function sqwarer(nombre) {
28    return nombre * nombre;
29  }
30
31  // And now the nombre splitte hymself
32  // So oone and tweye results from twelfe.
33  function ooneFoldeNombres(nombre) {
34    return String(nombre).split('').map(Number);
35  }
```

This is vintage Chaucer; in fact, it reads like an abbreviated version of *The Canterbury Tales*. As with that sprawling masterpiece, this solution is told by several protagonists in addition to the general narrator. (The Summoner and The Sqwarer—also pronounced "squire"—might have been lifted directly from his earlier work, but we'll let that go.)

The overall effect is oddly functional: Notice how the general narrator speaks in declarative terms (`summonTheSqwares`), and indeed there are no side effects that I can see. It's probably no coincidence that *The Canterbury Tales* is equally unimperative; Chaucer pays little attention to the passage of time and place—his primary interest is in the characters and their stories.

Here's a brief glossary for those of us who didn't pay attention in Middle English class:

Befil To befall, to happen

Eich-ian Reference to Brendan Eich, creator of JavaScript

Condicioun Condition

Parfit Perfect

Nombre Number

Summon the Sqwares Sum the squares

Oother Other

Summoner One who sums, also a character in *The Canterbury Tales*

Sqwarer One who squares, also alludes to the Squire in *The Canterbury Tales*

Oone One

Tweye Two

Acht Eight

Nyne Nine

Oonefolde To unfold, to split

I don't think in any language. I think in JavaScript.

VLADIMIR NABOKOV

1899–1977

Vladimir Nabokov is best known for Humbert Humbert's slippery account of his obsession with 12-year-old Lolita, but he should perhaps be better known as a lingual aesthete without peer.

Nabokov delights in fun and games, repurposing every fragment of each cleverly woven plot as a lexical playground for puns and anagrams, double entendres and almost-words, alliteration and acrostics. Yet those who dismiss Nabokov as merely a peddler of deftly chiseled whimsy overlook his ability to move or unnerve readers through vivid imagery. Here he summons a procession of sibilant *S*s, rugged *R*s, and bouncing *B*s to render a wistful picture of childhood contentment:

> *A sense of security, of well-being, of summer warmth pervades my memory. That robust reality makes a ghost of the present. The mirror brims with brightness; a bumblebee has entered the room and bumps against the ceiling.*[1]

Then there's his extraordinary gift for surface and sensory minutiae: a snowflake settling on the crystal glass of a wristwatch, the reflection from a bedstead, the suggestion of human speech in the echo of running tap water. To Nabokov, the "divine detail" is everything: "the capacity to wonder at trifles ... these asides of the spirit, these footnotes in the volume of life are the highest forms of consciousness, and it is in this childishly speculative state of mind, so different from commonsense and its logic, that we know the world to be good."[2]

An endless supply of germane metaphors applies texture to every nuance. This passage from *Pnin* conveys the harrowing fallout of a dental visit:

> *His tongue, a fat sleek seal, used to flop and slide so happily among the familiar rocks, checking the contours of a battered but still secure kingdom, plunging from cave to cove, climbing this jag, nuzzling that notch, finding a shred of sweet seaweed in the same old cleft; but now not a landmark remained, and all there existed was a great dark wound, a terra incognita of gums which dread and disgust forbade one to investigate.*[3]

Nabokov's highly original perspective on the everyday is extraordinarily funny. So is his mockery of the overearnest and the pretentious. Perhaps more than anyone, Nabokov believed in the thing for the sake of the thing; he had no time for the "literature of ideas" and held didacts in contempt. As Conrad Brenner wrote in the *New Republic*, "Humor becomes a swathe blighting all those falsely heavy approaches to life and literature, disclosing by the way its own irresistible angles. The strength of Nabokov lies in the check (and balance) of the sinister obbligato."[4]

Nabokov is a writer in complete control. Words are his minions; characters, as he famously put it, are his "galley slaves." And we, the readers, are probably just there for his amusement.

```
1   /*
2   In Pergatorya, our oblivious integer necessitated emotional validation by
3   means of a dubious algorithm of doubtful provenance. What followed was
4   a self-penned scryptogram exhibiting the unhappy confluence of mechanical
5   pedantry and digital peasantry. (Code is a bore to describe; yet a few basic
6   details are, reluctantly, given.)
7   */
8
9   function isItHappy(ourNumber) {
10    var terra, antiterra;
11    while (true) {
12      var terra = theNextNumber(terra || ourNumber);
13      var antiterra = theNextNumber(theNextNumber(antiterra || ourNumber));
14      if (terra == 1 || antiterra == 1) {
15        //Happiness: a temerarious tonsil tripping down the mouth
16        //to thrust, at three, against the palate.
17        //Hap. Ee. Ness.
18        return true;
19      }
20      if (terra == antiterra) {
21        //(history repeats) terra, antiterra, terror!
22        return false;
23      }
24    }
25  }
26
27  function theNextNumber(thisNumber) {
28    //being concolorus with the outcome...
29    var ourResult = 0;
30    //trying not to imagine the disasters inherent herein...
31    thisNumber.toString().split('').map(function(aDigit) {
32      return aDigit * aDigit;
33    }).forEach(function(aSquaredDigit) {
34      ourResult += aSquaredDigit;
35    });
36    return ourResult;
37  }
```

Nabokov's version of English is all his own, and so it is with his JavaScript.

So what on earth is going on here? Or should we ask what on *earths*? Because the keys to Nabokov's solution are *Terra* and *Antiterra*, the twin worlds of his grandiose masterpiece *Ada*. Terra resembles our earth, while Antiterra merely almost resembles it, being shifted in time and divergent of history.

Yes, yes, you ask, but what actually is going on here? Okay, remember how Holden Caulfield dispenses with history? Well, so does Nabokov (being famously wary of conventional wisdom's tyranny). And how? By running two happy numbers puzzles simultaneously—one on Terra, the other on Antiterra. Since Antiterra spins a little faster than Terra, it looks ahead a little farther each time. Now, if Terra and Antiterra should ever elicit the same response at the same time, we know in advance that history has repeated itself, and must therefore be looping. At this point the game is up, and we declare the hapless number unhappy.

On the other hand, should we be fortunate enough to reach numeric ecstasy, Nabokov will reprise the famous opening line of *Lolita*, only this time the exacting glossopharyngeal instruction is amended to form the word *happiness*.

And that's that. Though I admit I'm still scanning the code for evidence of further riddling . . .

The

REFACTOR

after "Do not go gentle into that good night"
by Dylan Thomas

Do not go gentle into that rewrite,
Good code should factor well at close of day;
Rage, rage against the gnarliness and blight.

Though sage minds craft their logic late at night,
Because it reads like forked spaghetti, they
Do not go gentle into that rewrite.

Brave Model View exponents, burning bright;
Their layers become lasagna down the way;
Rage, rage against the gnarliness and blight.

Bold men who mostly think in black and white,
Then learn, at last, to think in shades of grey,
Do not go gentle into that rewrite.

Tired heads, near death, who work with failing sight
Step back and move beyond this tangled fray,
Rage, rage against the gnarliness and blight.

And you, dear reader, faithful acolyte,
Audaciously address this sad decay.
Do not go gentle into that good rewrite.
Rage, rage against the gnarliness and blight.

PRIME N

THE ASSIGNMENT:
WRITE A FUNCTION THAT
RETURNS ALL THE PRIME
NUMBERS UP TO THE VALUE
OF THE SUPPLIED ARGUMENT.

A prime number is a positive integer that is divisible only by 1 and itself. Thus, 2 and 3 are prime numbers, but 4 isn't, because it's also divisible by 2. Here are the first 15 prime numbers:

2, 3, 5, 7, 11, 13, 17, 19, 23, 29, 31, 37, 41, 43, 47

UMBERS

There are no known formulae for calculating the full distribution of prime numbers. At the time of writing, the largest known prime was $2^{57,885,161} - 1$. The Electronic Frontier Foundation offers prizes for discovering very large primes.

Writing JavaScript and not writing JavaScript
is the only way I have to measure time.

JORGE LUIS BORGES

1899–1986

The restrained elegance of Jorge Luis Borges's phrasing stands in contrast to his fanciful imagery and wild, boundless imagination. Borges was a free spirit who followed his multiple obsessions (time, the universe, labyrinths, spaces) with unrestrained zeal and then transcribed them into simple, classically crafted prose.

Borges always maintained that he was a reader at heart, sharing Nabokov's fierce belief in reading for reading's sake. He dismissed the importance of meaning or message ("I don't intend to show anything. I have no intentions"[1]). The purpose of a book, Borges insisted, is aesthetic pleasure; a writer should be judged "by the enjoyment he gives and by the emotions one gets."[2]

Borges never wrote a full-length novel; he felt they were unworthy of the effort: "The composition of vast books is a laborious and impoverishing extravagance. To go on for five hundred pages developing an idea whose perfect oral exposition is possible in a few minutes!"[3] Instead, he concocted vast imaginary books and made them the subject of his short stories. "Tlön, Uqbar, Orbis Tertius" describes a fake encyclopedia for a made-up planet, the discovery of which triggers

an unstoppable wave of imitation that gradually wipes out all existing cultures. "The Garden
of Forking Paths" cites a sprawling and chaotic
novel in which each protagonist embarks on all
possible courses of action simultaneously, form-
ing an infinite network of temporal paths that
occasionally converge at points in the future.

In "The Library of Babel," Borges tells of an
endless array of identical hexagonal rooms, all
containing 20 shelves, each of which is stocked
with 32 identically bound 410-page books. At
some point in history, a "librarian of genius"
deduced that, since no two books are alike and
all books are formed from a random assortment
of the same characters, the library must contain
every book ever written and every book that
will ever be written.[4] In an uncanny nod to the
not-yet-invented Internet, the library's patrons
gradually realize that their ultimate treasure trove
of knowledge is in fact an infinite universe of
almost entirely useless data.

Borges was also an acclaimed poet. Although
his poems incorporate many of his favorite
themes, they tend to be more personal than his
stories, full of vulnerability and romantic angst.

```
1   // They speak (I know) of finials, newels and balustrades
2   // of hidden spandrels and eternally clambering, broad-gaited beasts...
3
4   var monstersAscendingAStaircase = function(numberOfSteps) {
5     var stairs = []; stepsUntrodden = [];
6     var largestGait = Math.sqrt(numberOfSteps);
7
8     // A succession of creatures mount the stairs;
9     // each creature's stride exceeds that of its predecessor.
10    for (var i = 2; i <= largestGait; i++) {
11      if (!stairs[i]) {
12        for (var j = i * i; j <= numberOfSteps; j += i) {
13          stairs[j] = 'stomp';
14        }
15      }
16    }
17
18    // Long-limbed monsters won't tread on prime-numbered stairs.
19    for (var i = 2; i <= numberOfSteps; i++) {
20      if (!stairs[i]) {
21        stepsUntrodden.push(i);
22      }
23    }
24
25    // Here, then, is our answer.
26    return stepsUntrodden;
27  };
```

Borges's solution combines several of his favorite motifs: mathematical theory, the geometric arrangement of spaces, a suggestion of infinity, and a story within a story. This is classic Borges: a narrator—who, in his excitement, possibly overplays the staircase imagery—tells of a mysterious book (*Monsters Ascending a Staircase*), and within a few short lines, we're right there living it.

As we watch the dogged procession of upwardly mobile monsters, we can't help wondering when Borges will get to the math part. Predictably, it turns out we were already there; the rank of the stair represents the numerator, and each monster's stride the denominator. Stairs that remain unstomped have no divisors and are thus primes. By transporting us to this imaginary world, Borges creates a distraction from the raw mechanics of prime numbers, while simultaneously illustrating how utterly simple, and universal, they are.

Borges's logic is clean and well organized, and his JavaScript straightforward and free from unnecessary cleverness, as befits his dislike for syntactic filigree. Yet, by dint of a few well-chosen comments and variable names, he achieves a glorious otherworldly effect.

"What is the use of JavaScript," thought Alice,
"without pictures or conversations?"

LEWIS CARROLL

1832–1898

Lewis Carroll was an esteemed mathematician, a pioneering photographer, a philosopher, and an Anglican deacon, but he is best known for his fanciful nonsense stories.

Alice's Adventures in Wonderland is a remarkable piece of escapist literature that influenced works as diverse as *Finnegans Wake* and *The Matrix*. For all its suggested allegory and academic allusions, what makes Alice a classic is the sheer, unapologetic madness of it all. Written in an era when children's fiction was dominated by stodgy morality tales, the plot of Alice couldn't be more refreshing: Bored Alice falls down a rabbit hole and hangs out with a menagerie of lovable crazies. When a creature speaks gibberish or acts peculiarly (which is most of the time), Carroll doesn't try to rationalize its behavior, as his contemporaries might have; instead, the reader is permitted to revel in absurdity for its own sake. Here's a quintessentially harebrained exchange from the mad tea party:

> *"What a funny watch!" [Alice] remarked. "It tells the day of the month, and doesn't tell what o'clock it is!"*
>
> *"Why should it?" muttered the Hatter. "Does your watch tell you what year it is?"*
>
> *"Of course not," Alice replied very readily: "but that's because it stays the same year for such a long time together."*

> *"Which is just the case with mine," said the Hatter.*
>
> *Alice felt dreadfully puzzled. The Hatter's remark seemed to have no sort of meaning in it, and yet it was certainly English. "I don't quite understand you," she said, as politely as she could.*
>
> *"The Dormouse is asleep again," said the Hatter, and he poured a little hot tea upon its nose.*[1]

The creatures of Wonderland are consistently rude to Alice, and though in over her head (literally) and generally uneasy about the whole situation, she never loses her dignity and always gives as good as she gets. Much humor is derived from this dynamic—the creatures' mild disdain for Alice is matched by her gentle contempt for them.

The sequel, *Through the Looking-Glass, and What Alice Found There*, is essentially a game of chess played on the other side of Alice's bedroom mirror. It features the beloved nonsense poem "Jabberwocky," which is written in mirrored text and peppered with made-up words, some of which (notably, the portmanteau *chortle*) have made it into everyday speech.

```
1   function downTheRabbitHole(growThisBig) {
2     var theFullDeck = Array(growThisBig);
3     var theHatter = Function('return this/4').call(2*2);
4     var theDuchess = Boolean("The frumious Bandersnatch!");
5
6     var theVerdict = "the white rabbit".split(/the march hare/).slice(theHatter);
7
8     //into the pool of tears...
9     eval (theFullDeck.join("if (!theFullDeck[++theHatter]) {\
10        theDuchess = 1;\
11        theVerdict.push(theHatter);\
12        " + theFullDeck.join("theFullDeck[++theDuchess * theHatter]=true;") + "}")
13    );
14
15    return theVerdict;
16  }
```

JavaScript is an unconventional language, brimming with charming quirks and hidden features. Over the years developers have embraced this kookiness, recognizing it as a vehicle for creativity and channeling it to make beautiful things. Recently, however, some developers, ashamed of its bizarre nature, have tried to reinvent JavaScript as a mainstream language—questioning the value of more esoteric features and lamenting that anyone should have to understand them.

Lewis Carroll is clearly on the liberal side of the debate; in fact, he's gone out of his way to make his JavaScript as oddball as possible. `theHatter` (which, I think, is intended as a loose pun on `theFactor`) is initialized by means of the rarely used `Function` constructor and the much-feared `this` keyword, and he jumps through (croquet) hoops to assign an empty array to `theVerdict`. Meanwhile, the setting of `theDuchess` (a play on words suggesting `theCount`?) to the Jabberwocky-esque *frumious Bandersnatch* is a pure red herring (the value of `theDuchess` is reassigned a couple of lines later).

But the coup de grâce is Carroll's use of the much-maligned but ridiculously powerful `eval` statement. Carroll ingeniously collapses a whole mass of code into a few lines by using `join` as an iterator, shoehorning the logic into the voids between each array element. Finally, he uses `eval` to execute (Queen of Hearts–style) the generated string, which by now is as long as the mouse's tail and as mad as a March hare.

JavaScript! Don't talk to me about JavaScript!

DOUGLAS ADAMS

1952–2001

When Douglas Adams approached the BBC with a proposal for a comedy radio series called *The Ends of the Earth*, his writing career was in the doldrums and he'd moved back in with his mother to make ends meet. That series became *The Hitchhiker's Guide to the Galaxy*, and it spawned five novels, a television series, a stage show, a computer game, a movie, and a comic-book series.

The *Hitchhiker's Guide* is a rollicking interstellar odyssey featuring unassuming earthling Arthur Dent and a disparate array of mostly nonhumanoid acquaintances. The book, which has achieved cult status among science fiction lovers, doubles as a vehicle for Adams to off-load an endless Monty Python–esque stream of wry and witty observations about life, the universe, and everything. In this excerpt from the first book, Adams ponders human intelligence:

> *For instance, on the planet Earth, man had always assumed that he was more intelligent than dolphins because he had achieved so much—the wheel, New York, wars and so on—whilst all the dolphins had ever done was muck about in the water having a good time. But conversely, the dolphins had always believed that they were far more intelligent than man—for precisely the same reasons.*[1]

To some extent, Adams's comic genius actually works against the book; Adams describes himself as "essentially a frivolous" writer, and much of the plot feels like filler in service of his clever one-liners.[2] There are other problems: The only obviously female character (and the only human besides Arthur) is Trillian, whom we are told (several times) is both exceptionally clever and exceptionally beautiful. Her character seems way too perfect for a mere humanoid, and yet for all her prowess, she's given very little to do.

Eventually, Adams burned out ("It felt like a mouse on a wheel; there was no pleasure coming into the cycle at any point"[3]) and turned to fresh endeavors, starting with the fantasy detective novel *Dirk Gently's Holistic Detective Agency* (built upon unused *Doctor Who* scripts), which spawned a sequel, *The Long Dark Tea-Time of the Soul*.

One of his final projects was the acclaimed radio series and nonfiction book *Last Chance to See*, in which Adams traveled to far-flung locations to hang out with animals on the brink of extinction. Fittingly, Adams described *Last Chance to See* as his favorite work.

```
1   //Here I am, brain the size of a planet, and they ask me to write JavaScript...
2   function kevinTheNumberMentioner(_){
3     l=[]
4   /* mostly harmless --> */ with(l) {
5
6       //Sorry about all this, my babel fish has a headache today...
7       for (ll=!+[]+!![];ll<_+(+!![]);ll++) {
8         lll=+!![];
9         while (ll%++lll);
10        //I've got this terrible pain in all the semicolons down my right-hand side.
11        (ll==lll)&&push(ll);
12      }
13      forEach(alert);
14
15    }
16
17    //You're really not going to like this...
18    return [!+[]+!+[]+!+[]+!+[]]+[!+[]+!+[]];
19  }
```

Adams's prime-number solution features contributions from some of his most beloved brainchildren. For instance, the opening comment drips with the doleful sarcasm of Marvin, the amusingly depressed robot (who, ironically, embodies the darker side of the human condition more than any of *Hitchhiker*'s organic characters). Later on, Marvin moans about his aching semicolons.

Meanwhile, the code itself represents the bizarre transmissions of a babel fish, the curious ear-dwelling creature that conveniently excretes nerve signals in the language of its host. Sadly, it seems this particular fish had a sore head, and so had a limited range of characters at its disposal. Adams apologizes for the fish's decidedly un-JavaScripty transcript, but no matter: It turns out everything works just fine. Notice, by the way, the use of the ever-controversial `with` statement, which sends narrow-minded earthlings running for cover but is considered "mostly harmless" by those with a more rational, pan-galactic perspective.

In another unusual twist, the generated prime numbers, instead of being returned en masse at the end of the program, are called out one by one by means of an `alert`. This clears the way for the grand finale, in which the bashful supercomputer Deep Thought announces to a hushed audience the answer to the life, the universe, and everything. But, alas, it's 42 (in sick babel fish parlance).

It was the best of languages, it was the worst of languages.

CHARLES DICKENS

1812–1870

The most celebrated English novelist of the 19th century, and still immensely popular today, Charles Dickens wrote 19 novels, none of which has ever gone out of print.

Most of Dickens's fiction was originally published in monthly installments—in magazines or as crudely bound, standalone pamphlets. Since each installment was relatively cheap, his stories were available to those of lesser means, which provided Dickens with a receptive audience for his accounts of social injustice. Damning portraits of villainous landowners and belligerent factory owners were juxtaposed, as never before, with vivid depictions of the destitution and squalor in London's wretched underbelly.

Dickens ended each installment with a cliffhanger—an unresolved misfortune or unexplained revelation—so as to beef up anticipation for the next issue. Famously, as Little Nell's condition deteriorated, crowds in New York gathered on the wharf shouting, "Is Nell dead?!" to the crew of the vessel delivering the next installment of *The Old Curiosity Shop.*

Everything about Dickens's characters is larger than life, starting with their names. In Dickens's world, names are invariably a window into their owners' personalities, whether via onomatopoeia (*Martin Chuzzlewit*, *Mercy Pecksniff*, *Polly Toodle*), portmanteau (*Mr. Murdstone*, *Lawrence Boythorn*, *Mr. Tulkinghorn*), or metaphor (*Mealy Potatoes*, *Mr. Smallweed*, *Clarence Barnacle*). Dickens assigns idiosyncrasies and affectations to great comic effect and uses his exceptional flair for dialect to designate education, social status, and morality.

Dickens's talent for portraying good and evil is to some extent his undoing. Whereas the best fiction recognizes that there is grace and ugliness in each of us, and exploits that conflict for dramatic effect, Dickens's tendency to paint almost every character as either victim or villain limits our ability to identify with any of them. Then again, his lively writing, wonderful dialog, and eloquent fusing of dark and comic themes may be compensation enough.

```
1   function MrsPrimmerwicksProgeny(MaxwellNumberby) {
2
3     Number.prototype.isAPrimmerwick = function() {
4      for (var AddableChopper = 2; AddableChopper <= this; AddableChopper++) {
5       var BittyRemnant = this % AddableChopper;
6       if (BittyRemnant == 0 && this != AddableChopper) {
7        return console.log(
8          "It is composite. The dear, gentle, patient, noble", +this, "is composite."),
9           false;
10       }
11      }
12      return console.log(
13        "Oh,", +this, +this, +this, "what a happy day this is for you and me!"),
14          true;
15     }
16
17     var VenerableHeap = [];
18     for (var AveryNumberby = 2; AveryNumberby <= MaxwellNumberby; AveryNumberby++) {
19      if (AveryNumberby.isAPrimmerwick()) {
20       VenerableHeap.push(AveryNumberby);
21      }
22     }
23     return VenerableHeap;
24   }
```

A master of overstatement, Dickens forms a solution that is nothing if not thorough. Instead of using a standalone prime-number utility, he chooses to augment `Number.prototype` so that the very numbers may discover their primeness for themselves. Regardless of the outcome, we're treated to a gushing display of Dickens's trademark sentimentality. When a number is composite (i.e., not prime), Dickens layers on the pathos, Little Nell–style, so that even the most coldhearted among us would be apt to choke up.[1] When the number is prime, the syrupy cheer is worthy of the Cheeryble brothers.[2]

```
> MrsPrimmerwicksProgeny(6)
Oh, 2 2 2 what a happy day this is for you and me!
Oh, 3 3 3 what a happy day this is for you and me!
It is a composite. The dear, gentle, patient, noble 4 is a composite.
Oh, 5 5 5 what a happy day this is for you and me!
It is a composite. The dear, gentle, patient, noble 6 is a composite.
[2, 3, 5]
```

(Note how Dickens uses `+this` to represent the number; `this` represents the number as an object, and + coerces it to its primitive value. He also uses the comma operator to return a Boolean value after console-logging his sentimental bilge.)

As usual, Dickens uses wacky character names to full effect. `AddableChopper` is an incremental divisor to `BittyRemnant`'s waif-like remainder. `MaxwellNumberby` is the biggest number to test for; `AveryNumberby` represents every value in the iteration. `VenerableHeap` is Uriah's less obsequious twin brother—he's responsible for delivering the result.

Beauty is not the goal of JavaScript,
but JavaScript is a prime venue for
the expression of beauty.

DAVID FOSTER WALLACE

1962–2008

Recalling a vacation in Hawaii, David Foster Wallace's widow, Karen Green, noted that while she swam in the ocean, Wallace stood on the shore "yelling anecdotal statistics about shark attacks."[1] This obsessive personality is the key to Wallace's distinctive approach to writing. His heavy use of endnotes and footnotes is not a literary gimmick but an earnest (and to Wallace's mind, necessary) attempt to include every relevant detail without disrupting the narrative flow. Similarly, Wallace's snail-paced plot development owes more to obsession than to patience; while most authors are anxious to keep the story moving, Wallace feels duty-bound to stay with a scene for as long as he has something to say about it.

In Wallace's prose, the highbrow and the vernacular routinely rub shoulders in the same sentence, and phrases oscillate between well crafted and deliberately sloppy. Sentences sometimes stretch for hundreds of words with minimal punctuation, and in another nod to obsession, Wallace is apt to repeat himself or restate the protagonist's identity for the sake of clarity. The following sentence fragment from one of his short stories includes several characteristic Wallacisms.

> *. . . which, when X rejoins that for Christ's sweet sake this is what he's already been doing all along, Y tentatively pats his (i.e., X's) shoulder and ventures to say that X has always struck him (=Y) as a good deal stronger and wiser and more compassionate than he, X, is willing to give himself credit for.*[2]

Wallace completed only two novels. The first, *The Broom of the System*, was submitted as part of his undergraduate thesis. The second, *Infinite Jest*, is a 1,078-page treatise on addiction and alienation in near-future America.

Infinite Jest begins with a white-knuckle account of an admissions interview gone wrong. It's tight, beautifully crafted, and visceral ("The familiar feeling of being misperceived is rising, and my chest bumps and thuds"[3]). From there, things break down as Wallace presents us with a series of fragmented vignettes and loosely related portraits, until gradually, miraculously, a thread of plot emerges. *Infinite Jest* is many things: parody, fantasy, political thriller—at a high level, it's even a mathematical exercise—but these are not the qualities that define its greatness. Rather, it's the compassion with which Wallace articulates the plight of the desolate and the desperate, and his jaw-dropping eloquence, which instills a sense of wonder in the everyday.

```
1    var yearOfTheLightningQuickAtkinSieve = function(tops){
2    //B.P. #40 07-14
3    //ELEPHANT BUTTE, NM
4    var NSRS/*[1]*/ = [0,0,2,3];
5    /* One of those klutzy sort of bad-taste-in-the-mouth concurrent looping devices
     so that two variables (i and j, both initially 1) are incremented
     gradum-ad-tempus[2]. */
6    for (var i = 1; i < Math.sqrt(tops); i++){
7      for (var j = 1; j < Math.sqrt(tops); j++){
8        /* The two variables (i.e. i and j) are implanted in the first quadratic,
         while its (the quadratic's) disgorgement is fed to a third variable, n. */
9        var n = 4*i*i + j*j;
10       /* If dividing this latest variable (i.e. n) by 12 upchucks a remainder
         of 1 or 5, the value at that index (i.e. n's) is flipped[3].*/
11       if ((n <= tops) && ((n%12 == 1) || (n%12 == 5))){
12         NSRS[n] = NSRS[n] ? 0 : n;
13       }
14       /* Now, we (i.e. JavaScript) reach the second quadratic and again the result
         is piped to the (already used once) variable n. */
15       n = 3*i*i + j*j;
16       /* Although the variable (i.e. n) is again divided by 12, this time a
         remainder of 7 is enough to make the indexed value (i.e. the value at n)
         flip. Not well understood. */
17       if ((n <= tops) && (n % 12 == 7)){
18         NSRS[n] = NSRS[n] ? 0 : n;
19       }
20       /* By now you (i.e. the reader) are no doubt experiencing feelings of
         ambivalence and/or regret; nevertheless, we (i.e. JavaScript) haven't
         finished yet. Predictably, a third quadratic is now run and (equally
         predictably) its value assigned to the (now world-weary) variable, n. */
21       n = 3*i*i - j*j;
22       /* The only interesting thing about the third division (though also the
         depressing thing) is that it only happens when the first looping variable
         (i) is greater than i.e. not less than (or equal to) the second looping
         variable (j)[4][5]. */
23       if (i>j) {
```

```
24        if ((n <= tops) && (n % 12 == 11)){
25          NSRS[n] = NSRS[n] ? 0 : n;
26        }
27      }
28    }
29  }
30  /* Near exhaustion (yet distrustful of the Quadratic Wheel Factorization Filter)
    we (i.e. JavaScript) now designate any and all prime factors, w/o regard for
    their current prime, or composite (i.e. non-prime) designation, as being
    composite (i.e non-prime) */
31  for (i = 5; i < Math.sqrt(tops); i++){
32    if (NSRS[i] == 1){
33      for (j = i*i; j < tops; j += i*i){
34        NSRS[j] = 0;
35      }
36    }
37  }
38  return NSRS.filter(Number); //[6]
39 }
40 /*
   [1] Numeric Storage and Retrieval System.
   [2] One step at a time.
   [3] Meaning values representing the current index are set to 0, while values of 0
   are set to the current index.
   [4] Otherwise, each relevant index[a] would be flipped twice.
   [5] Also some shady business with remainder 11. But enough already.
   [6] `Array.prototype.filter` being a higher-order function defined by the
   EcmaScript-262 Standard (5th edition) clause 15.4.4.20[b]. Since `Number` is a
   built-in function that converts any value to a number and Array.prototype.filter
   rejects "falsey" (i.e. not "truthy") values, thus values of 0, being "falsey"
   (i.e. not "truthy") will not be included in the array returned by
   `Array.prototype.filter`. If that makes sense.

   [a] i.e. a value of n for which the quadratic in question resolves to true.
   [b] http://es5.github.io/#x15.4.4.20. All right edition 5.1 but who's counting (no
   question mark).
   */
```

Wallace is on familiar ground here: As an undergraduate he studied modal logic and mathematics, and later he wrote a book about infinity.[4] Moreover, in a 1996 radio interview, Wallace claimed he modeled *Infinite Jest* after the Sierpinski gasket, "which is a very primitive kind of pyramidal fractal."[5]

In the same interview (and perhaps still alluding to fractals), Wallace observes that much of modern intellectual life is about building relationships between discreet pieces of information, so it's not hard to see why his algorithm of choice is the Sieve of Atkin, a series of apparently arbitrary logical fragments that together form a highly efficient prime-number generator.

As a post-postmodern author who rejects serial irony as tedious and unconstructive, Wallace approaches the problem with honest enthusiasm. (You can be pretty certain he devoured the entire ECMAScript standard before he wrote a line of code.) Such is his passion for explanatory detail that he very nearly drowns his JavaScript in a sea of characteristically DFW-esque annotations.

Oh, and the title `yearOfTheLightningQuick-AtkinSieve` is a nod to *Infinite Jest*, wherein chapters are named for calendar years, and calendar years are named for the highest bidder.

O CAPTAIN, MY Captain

after "O Captain! My Captain!"
by Walt Whitman

O CAPTAIN! my Captain! our application's done;

The code has weather'd every hack, the prize we sought is won;

The end is near, and now I hear my coworkers exulting,

With cheerful cries, they bid goodbye to code reviews and pairing:

But O heart! heart! heart!

O the nagging sense of dread,

For late last night I ran the tests,

And some of them were red.

THE ASSIGNMENT:

WRITE A CHAINABLE FUNCTION THAT ACCEPTS ONE WORD PER FUNCTION CALL BUT, WHEN CALLED WITHOUT ARGUMENTS, WILL REPORT BACK ALL THE PREVIOUSLY PASSED WORDS IN ORDER.

Finally, a nonmathematical exercise! A chainable function is one whose return value is itself a function so that repeated calls can be chained in a single statement.

SAY IT

Here's `sayIt` demonstrating its chainable credentials:

```
sayIt('hello')('my')('name')('is')
('Arundhati')();
```

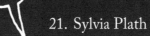

The final call passes no arguments, which tells `sayIt` it's time to cough up this message:

`"hello my name is Arundhati"`

If you expect nothing from JavaScript,
you're never disappointed.

SYLVIA PLATH

---◆▪━●━●━●━◆▪■◆---

1932–1963

It's hard to separate Sylvia Plath's writing from her troubled life. Plath's suicide at age 30 more or less defined the public's perception of her oeuvre: desperate, angry, and uncompromising—the so-called *confessional* voice. Yet by her own admission, Plath hid behind many masks, and it was only at the very end of her life that she fully allowed the constant feelings of hurt, alienation, and terror to flood unchecked onto the page. Most of the work for which she's now famous was published posthumously.

Plath dared to hope that her marriage to the British poet Ted Hughes ("the only man in the world who is my match") would bury her lifelong demons.[1] Five years after their wedding, Plath and Hughes gave a rare interview to the BBC in which Plath attempts to convey a rosy picture of housewifely life and nonchalantly recalls a childhood battle with depression as though it were now just a footnote.[2] In fact, as her journal would later relate, their marriage was by then quite troubled, and the cracks in Plath's psyche were as deep as ever.

The following year, after Plath confirmed that her husband was having an affair with their tenant, the couple separated. Plath channeled her despair into unparalleled creativity. Now all masks were discarded, and with gushing rage, she perfected the language of her torment. The so-called October poems—"Ariel," "Daddy," and

"Lady Lazarus"—written in the first month after the separation, are raw, visceral, and devastating. In "Lady Lazarus," Plath announces her impending suicide while chiding the voyeuristic public from whom she feels so alienated:

> *This is Number Three.*
> *What a trash*
> *To annihilate each decade.*
>
> *What a million filaments.*
> *The peanut-crunching crowd*
> *Shoves in to see*
>
> *Them unwrap me hand and foot—*
> *The big strip tease.*
> *Gentlemen, ladies* [3]

It ends with a cry of vengeance and a promise of rebirth:

> *Herr God, Herr Lucifer*
> *Beware*
> *Beware.*
>
> *Out of the ash*
> *I rise with my red hair*
> *And I eat men like air.*

Three months after writing "Lady Lazarus," Plath was found dead at her home.

```javascript
1   words = ''; wordless=' ';
2   // I am calm. I am calm.
3   function say_it(word) {
4     //It is the calm before something awful.
5     return word ? smothered_mouthfuls(word) : end();
6   }
7
8   function smothered_mouthfuls(word) {
9     // Dutifully swallowing words
10    word = words ? wordless + word : word;
11    words = words + word;
12    return say_it;
13  }
14
15  function end() {
16    // Grudgingly, my ungainly tongue
17    // Pokes and stirs, to render
18    // Empty substanceless nothings
19    return void this, words;
20  }
```

Characteristically, Plath's code is written in free verse, and there is a generous smattering of adverbs in the comments. As the verses unfold, we see echoes of Plath's own experience.

The opening verse contains the ternary expression on which the entire solution balances: Only in silence will words be spoken. This unsettling tone brings about a familiar sense of foreboding.

Next, instead of being voiced, the word is stuffed into an airless string. Plath considers this quite sinister and names the function `smothered_mouthfuls` to convey her disdain. The inhumanity of the process is affirmed by the monotony of the middle couplet:

```
word = words ? wordless + word : word;
words = words + word;
```

Nor is there glory in the final stanza. Using the comma operator to shoehorn `void this` in front of the result has no practical purpose but serves to emphasize what Plath sees as the emptiness of the outcome. The words, interned beyond their useful life, have lost their purpose and come out wrong, eerily echoing a sentiment from her own journal:

> *[Y]ou stop in shock at the words you utter— they are so rusty, so ugly, so meaningless and feeble from being kept in the small cramped dark inside you so long.* [4]

You'll understand JavaScript when you've forgotten what you understood before.

ITALO CALVINO

1923–1985

Italo Calvino was both a masterful storyteller and a literary innovator. Fearing the traditional novel had run its course, and feeling imprisoned by its boundaries, Calvino experimented obsessively with new forms. His early novels were mainstream, realist affairs, and although they were well received, he was deeply unsatisfied, both with the tedium of production and the end result. Here, in a letter to a friend, he explains his unhappiness:

> *The novel I was writing, which for months and months had sucked all my blood (because, stubborn as I am, I was determined to finish it even though I no longer felt it was going anywhere), is dead, awful, full of wonderful clever things but desperately bad, forced, it'll never work and I must not finish it.*[1]

Four years later, Calvino experienced a creative epiphany:

> *I began doing what came most naturally to me—that is, following the memory of the things I had loved best since boyhood. Instead of making myself write the book I ought to write, the novel that was expected of me, I conjured up the book I myself would have liked to read, the sort by an unknown writer, from another age and another country, discovered in an attic.*[2]

Calvino found his calling as a writer of postmodern fables. His breakthrough work, *The Cloven Viscount*, was written in just 30 days and chronicles the adventures of a nobleman who, literally split in half by a cannonball, continues to live as two separate people. Having found his voice, Calvino never looked back. He eagerly explored new forms—mathematical, symmetrical, self-referential—infusing each creation with a winsome cocktail of wit, badinage, and gentle melancholy.

Today, Calvino is best known for the metafictional *If on a Winter's Night a Traveler*, a nutty trompe l'oeil of a novel in which the author appears to bend the laws of nature by casting you, the reader, as the protagonist. Owing to a series of publishing errors, each alternate chapter is the beginning of an unrelated novel, and the book is an account of your vain attempt to read it. For all his shenanigans, Calvino never forgets that he is first and foremost a writer of stories. Each false start is a compelling tale, which, of course, leaves you wanting more.

```
1   function sayIt(word) {
2     var verse = '';
3     //If on a winter's night a programmer
4     return chapterOr(word, function chapter1(word) {
5       //outside the meaningful logic
6       return chapterOr(word, function chapter2(word) {
7         //leaning towards deep nests
8         return chapterOr(word, function chapter3(word) {
9           //without fear of callback vertigo
10          return chapterOr(word, function chapter4(word) {
11            //looks back at the gathering indents
12            return chapterOr(word, function chapter5(word) {
13              //in a network of functions that enlace
14              return chapterOr(word, function chapter6(word) {
15                //in a network of functions that stack
16                return chapterOr(word, function chapter7(word) {
17                  //on a carpet of illusions
18                  return chapterOr(word, function chapter8(word) {
19                    //around an empty core...
20                    return chapterOr(word, function chapter9(word) {
21                      //What story down there awaits its end?
22                      return chapterOr(word, chapter1);
23                    });
24                  });
25                });
26              });
27            });
28          });
29        });
30      });
31    });
32    function chapterOr(word, chapter) {
33      word && (verse += (verse && ' ') + word);
34      return word ? chapter : verse;
35    }
36  }
```

Calvino, for whom traditional software patterns are too limiting, has chosen to write his `sayIt` solution in the form of his self-referential masterpiece *If on a Winter's Night a Traveler*. And remarkably, it looks as if this daring gamble has paid off. Although the result is a little long-winded, there's an elegance and symmetry to the neatly nested routines, while the logic is breezy and uncluttered. Notice that each function (chapter) bears a comment that is a playful take on the corresponding chapter title in the original work.

On the face of it, nothing happens. Each function encloses another—deeper and deeper we go, opening functions like Russian dolls until we reach the core. Expecting an answer, we're instead redirected back to Chapter 1, and with exasperation we begin the cycle anew.

Cunningly, the meaningful part of the solution is squirreled away in the ostensibly trivial `chapterOr` function, which is invoked by each named chapter and offers up the next chapter or, when no word is passed, finally brings blessed relief in the form of an answer.

There's more to JavaScript than waving
your wand and saying a few funny words.

J.K.
ROWLING

1965–

While traveling from Manchester to London by train in 1990, Joanne Rowling dreamed up a story of a boy attending wizard school. Seven years later, *Harry Potter and the Philosopher's Stone*[1] was published under the name J.K. Rowling (apparently so as not to discourage male readers). It was the first volume of what became the best-selling book series in history.

Rowling is a masterful storyteller, crafting tight, intricate, highly imaginative plotlines and delivering them in simple, no-nonsense prose that is always articulate but never gets in the way. Her writing is also charming and funny, and her best character names (Albus Dumbledore, Cornelius Fudge, Severus Snape) are worthy of Thackeray and Dickens. And of course, there's magic by the bucketload!

Although never preachy or didactic, Rowling peppers the stories with morality tales. When Harry encounters Draco Malfoy in Madam Malkin's robe shop, he's repelled by Malfoy's prejudice. And Harry bitterly opposes the bigotry behind Professor Lupin's forced resignation from Hogwarts.

Given Rowling's considerable literary acumen, it's no surprise that she recently made a foray into novels for grown-ups, including the *Cormoran Strike* detective series written under the nom de plume Robert Galbraith.

```
1    function mumbleMore(pensieve, wormword, muggleBile, squib) {
2     var spells = {
3       engorgio: function (fn) {
4         //bind with pensieves, words, and muggleBile
5         return fn.bind(muggleBile, wormword ? pensieve.concat(wormword):[pensieve]);
6       },
7       accio: function (squib) {
8         //gather the pensieves
9         return pensieve.join(' ');
10      }
11    }
12
13    return spells[(wormword || pensieve.split) ? 'engorgio' : 'accio'](mumbleMore);
14  }
```

Most of the authors in this book prepared for their assignment by attending JavaScript school. Such is the wizardry of her solution, we can only assume that Rowling went the extra mile and enrolled at Hogwarts, too.

Rowling has called her solution `mumbleMore`, and like any competent magician, she begins by assembling the ingredients for the cauldron. `muggleBile` and `squib` are just there for flavor. The active ingredients are `wormword` (which usually represents the next word) and `pensieve` (a special memory device that Albus Dumbledore uses to store the array of words).

Next we see the recipes for the two spells Rowling will be using. They're both named for spells used in the Harry Potter books: `engorgio` (the engorgement charm) causes the subject—in this case, the pensieve of words—to swell in size, while `accio` (the summoning charm) recalls the pensieve's memory.

The first time `mumbleMore` is called, the word is assigned to the `pensieve`. Then `engorgio` creates a new function that magically bakes the current value of `pensieve` into its first argument. Thus, the next time `mumbleMore` is called, `pensieve` is already preset to an array of all previous words, and the new word is assigned to the `wormword` argument. Still following? No one said sorcery was easy!

This pattern repeats each time `mumbleMore` is called, until, eventually it's called without passing a word parameter. At this point `accio` steps in to join the `pensieve` into a long string—and there's your answer.

Gallopin' Gorgons!

There's no such thing as JavaScript.
Only JavaScript–shaped holes in the universe.

ARUNDHATI ROY

1961–

Arundhati Roy's 1997 debut novel, *The God of Small Things*, took the literary world by storm. A critical and popular triumph, it won the prestigious Booker Prize and became the best-selling novel by a resident Indian. We're still awaiting a second novel, but in the meantime, Roy has produced a steady stream of nonfiction. Most of it is politically themed, reflecting her anticorporate, pro-people, pro-environment philosophy.

The God of Small Things is a masterpiece. Set in the southwest Indian state of Kerala between 1969 and 1993, it's at once a profound indictment of the ingrained injustice of Roy's homeland, and a stunningly evocative prose poem. From the opening lines, Roy's writing dazzles:

> *May in Ayemenem is a hot, brooding month. The days are long and humid. The river shrinks and black crows gorge on bright mangoes in still, dustgreen trees. Red bananas ripen. Jackfruits burst. Dissolute bluebottles hum vacuously in the fruity air. Then they stun themselves against clear windowpanes and die, fatly baffled in the sun.*[1]

And so it continues—a haunting, sad, and eloquent treatise on the natural beauty of her home state, and the vulnerability and malevolence of humanity. Even as we recoil at the brutality of the caste system and despair at the hurt inflicted by family members turned bitter, the jaw-dropping beauty of Roy's writing threatens to upstage the horror of the events she describes. In this passage, we're told of Estha's retreat into a life of silence, brought about by the trauma of abuse and forced separation from his mother:

> *Once the quietness arrived, it stayed and spread in Estha. It reached out of his head and enfolded him in its swampy arms. It rocked him to the rhythm of an ancient, fetal heartbeat. It sent its stealthy, suckered tentacles inching along the insides of his skull, hoovering the knolls and dells of his memory; dislodging old sentences, whisking them off the tip of his tongue. It stripped his thoughts of the words that described them and left them pared and naked. Unspeakable. Numb. And to an observer therefore, perhaps barely there. Slowly, over the years, Estha withdrew from the world. He grew accustomed to the uneasy octopus that lived inside him and squirted its inky tranquilizer on his past. Gradually the reason for his silence was hidden away, entombed somewhere deep in the soothing folds of the fact of it.*[2]

The book's language is unorthodox. Roy confers new meanings on nouns and phrases (especially childhood creations) by capitalizing them. Many paragraphs are exceptionally short, sometimes only one word. The narration is technically third-person omniscient, but it makes frequent use of free indirect speech to assume the childhood perspective of twins Estha and, especially, Rahel (whose biography resembles the author's), so sentences routinely blend the mature adult voice with the singsong lilt and creative vocabulary of curious preteens:

> *The woman in the neighboring car had biscuit crumbs on her mouth. Her husband lit a bent after-biscuit cigarette. He exhaled two tusks of smoke through his nostrils and for a fleeting moment looked like a wild boar. Mrs. Boar asked Rahel her name in a Baby Voice.*[3]

For almost a decade, rumors of a second novel have abounded. In a recent *New York Times Magazine* piece, Roy confirmed she was indeed working on another novel (but said she's "keeping the subject secret for now").[4] We can only hope.

```
1   // 1) Start with the answer. 2) Move on to the Grubby Details.
2   // A viable try-able plan.
3   function sayIt(word) {
4
5     return TheSayItSaveItThing(word);
6
7     // Does Whatever-it-is-you-need-it-to.
8     // Loyal. Dependable. Weak-kneed.
9     function TheSayItSaveItThing(word) {
10      // When invoked it Saves.
11      KochuFunction(word);
12      // When addressed it Says.
13      TheSayItSaveItThing.toString = function() {
14        return TheStretchableFetchableThing.join(' ');
15      }
16      // Then it waits to be re-summoned.
17      // Not invoking. Not recursing. Just waiting.
18      return TheSayItSaveItThing;
19    }
20
21    // Why change KochuFunction when KochuFunction can change itself?
22    function KochuFunction(word) {
23      TheStretchableFetchableThing = [word];
24      KochuFunction = function(word) {
25        TheStretchableFetchableThing.push(word);
26      }
27      // KochuFunction is no longer what it was.
28      // Or thought it'd be. Ever.
29    }
30  }
```

The plot of *The God of Small Things* is non-linear, and so is Roy's JavaScript code. Just as the novel begins at the end and then fills in the gaps through a series of flashbacks, so the `sayIt` utility begins by returning the completed phrase before supplying the "Grubby Details." To this end, Roy's solution leans heavily on function declarations, which will be *hoisted* (moved to the top of the code) by the compiler.

With trademark elegance, Roy never once resorts to conditional logic. Her `KochuFunction` (*Kochu* is Malayalam for "little") makes use of the so-called *Russian doll pattern*, whereby after the function has been called once, it redefines itself.[5] So the first time `KochuFunction` is called, it creates a new array seeded by the given word, after which it reinvents itself as a function for pushing subsequent words onto the existing array.

Meanwhile, `TheSayItSaveItThing` returns whatever you need it to, without having to be told. If you call it with a word, the word gets stored. When you're done calling it, the function itself is returned and will, thanks to a crafty `toString` method, magically reveal the completed phrase.

Roy names her functions and variables from the perspective of the novel's young twins, while the comments resemble her typically haunting (yet playful) narrative.

Don't edit your JavaScript according to the fashion;
rather, follow your most intense obsessions mercilessly.

FRANZ
KAFKA

1883–1924

The popular image of Franz Kafka—the persecuted outsider, writing dark tales of doomed entrapment—is as shallow as it is misleading. Kafka's biographer and great friend Max Brod recalls a charming, calm, and funny man. Brod wrote of Kafka's "pleasure in art and his joy in creating"[1] and of his reading his work aloud to friends, sometimes laughing "so much that there were moments he could not read any further."[2] Moreover, an open-minded reading of his best-known works—*The Trial*, *The Castle*, and *The Metamorphosis*—reveals a rich vein of absurdist humor, and heroes who face adversity with both confidence and tenacity. Although he certainly had moments of profound despair, the real Kafka probably had little in common with the humorless, solitary, peddler-of-doom persona with which he is most often associated.

Some of these misperceptions can be traced to the early canonical translations of Kafka's work, which tended to gussy up the starkness of his original German to achieve a more literary cadence; sentences were shortened, repeated words replaced with synonyms, and formal expressions swapped for more lively colloquialisms. Later translators realized that most of Kafka's "mistakes" were most likely intentional; his unsophisticated narrative imparts a naive, almost disinterested quality that makes anomalies of plot seem more absurd than sinister.

The effect is often more Chaplinesque than Kafkaesque. In *The Trial*, Joseph K.'s escalating legal problems are affecting his work, so when he's asked to accompany a visiting Italian businessman on a sightseeing trip, it's imperative that he make a good impression. But disastrously, the Italian's mustache is too bushy for K. to make out what he's saying (and still, we're told that K. is so intrigued at the possibility the mustache might be perfumed that it's all he can do not to get close and take a sniff). In *The Metamorphosis*, Gregor Samsa is apparently less alarmed at having woken up in the body of a giant beetle than he is at the prospect of arriving to work late. The following excerpt culminates in one of literature's most brilliant understatements:

> *The next train left at seven o'clock. To catch that one, he would have to go in a mad rush. The sample collection wasn't packed up yet, and he really didn't feel particularly fresh and active.* [3]

The Metamorphosis illustrates how, despite (or maybe because of) Kafka's aversion to pathos, his writing can be very moving. Who else could make us shed tears for an outsized cockroach?

```
1   function sayIt(firstWord) {
2     var words = [];
3     return (function sayIt(word) {
4       if (!word) {
5         try {
6           return sayIt();
7         } catch (e) {
8           // quitting at last an unsettling recursion,
9           // the array was transformed into a monstrous string
10          words = "there's been a hideous bug";
11          return words;
12        }
13      } else {
14        words.push(word);
15        return sayIt;
16      }
17    })(firstWord);
18  }
```

It all seemed so promising. Kafka's solution, typically plain and lacking in ornamentation, looked robust enough. But running the code revealed a hideous bug, and there seems to be no way around it.

At first all went well. With each successive call to `sayIt`, the supplied word was added to the stored array. Simple enough, right? When it came time to return the list of words, we called `sayIt` without arguments. But then the function started reinvoking itself. Again and again.

Now we're recursing endlessly, with no hope of redemption. But wait, I think it's going to be okay after all because, look . . . we're catching the stack overflow exception. And yet, this is where things get very strange indeed; our array of words has somehow become a terrible and useless string. It's as though it were subject to some kind of metamorphosis . . .

And so, alas, Kafka's is the only solution in the book that does not successfully resolve itself.

Very Kafkaesque.

Notes

INTRODUCTION

1. Stephen Pinker, *The Language Instinct: How the Mind Creates Language (P.S.)* (New York: William Morrow and Company, 1994; New York: HarperCollins, 2007), 385. Page reference is to the HarperCollins edition.

2. Francis Bacon, "Of Beauty," *The Essaies of Sr Francis Bacon* (1613), *https://archive.org/details/essaiesofsrfranc00baco.*

HEMINGWAY

1. "Ernest Hemingway, The Art of Fiction No. 21," interview by George Plimpton, *Paris Review*, no. 18, Spring 1958, *http://www.theparisreview.org/interviews/4825/the-art-of-fiction-no-21-ernest-hemingway.*

BRETON

1. André Breton, "Facteur Cheval," trans. David Gascoyne, *Contemporary Poetry and Prose*, no. 2 (June 1936), 25–26, *http://www.jheilharz.de/surrealism/gascoyne-translations.html#breton.*

BOLAÑO

1. Roberto Bolaño, *The Unknown University*, trans. Laura Healy (New York: New Directions, 2013), 413.

2. Roberto Bolaño, *The Savage Detectives*, trans. Natasha Wimmer (Farrar, Straus and Giroux, 2007), 48.

BROWN

1. Janet Maslin, "Spinning a Thriller from a Gallery at the Louvre," *New York Times*, March 17, 2003, *http://www.nytimes.com/2003/03/17/books/books-of-the-times-spinning-a-thriller-from-a-gallery-at-the-louvre.html.*

2. A.O. Scott, "A 'Da Vinci Code' That Takes Longer to Watch Than Read," *New York Times*, May 18, 2006, *http://www.nytimes.com/2006/05/18/movies/18code.html.*

3. Anthony Lane, "Heaven Can Wait," *New Yorker*, May 29, 2006, *http://www.newyorker.com/archive/2006/05/29/060529crci_cinema.*

4. Dan Brown, *The Da Vinci Code* (New York: Doubleday, 2003; New York: Anchor Books, 2009), 3. Page reference is to the Anchor Books edition.

5. Geoffrey K. Pullum, "The Dan Brown Code," *Language Log* (blog), May 1, 2004, *http://itre.cis.upenn.edu/~myl/languagelog/archives/000844.html.*

6. Tom Chivers, "The Lost Symbol and The Da Vinci Code author Dan Brown's 20 worst sentences," *Telegraph*, September 15, 2009, *http://www.telegraph.co.uk/culture/books/booknews/6194031/The-Lost-Symbol-and-The-Da-Vinci-Code-author-Dan-Browns-20-worst-sentences.html.*

KEROUAC

1. Penny Vlagopoulos, online introduction to *On the Road: The Original Scroll* (New York: Penguin Books), *http://www.penguin.com/read/book-clubs/on-the-road-the-original-scroll/9780143105466.*

2. "Jack Kerouac, The Art of Fiction No. 41," interview by Ted Berrigan, *Paris Review*, no. 43, Summer 1968, *http://www.theparisreview.org/interviews/4260/the-art-of-fiction-no-41-jack-kerouac.*

3. Jack Kerouac, "Aftermath: The Philosophy of the Beat Generation," (1958) in *Good Blonde and Others*, ed. Donald Allen (San Francisco: Grey Fox Press, 1993), 47–50.

4. David Dempsey, review of *The Subterraneans*, by Jack Kerouac, *New York Times*, February 23, 1956, *http://www.nytimes.com/books/97/09/07/home/kerouac-subterraneans.html.*

5. Jack Kerouac, *The Subterraneans* (New York: Grove Press, 1958), 13.

6. Jack Kerouac, "Essentials of Spontaneous Prose," *Black Mountain Review*, 1957, *http://www.writing.upenn.edu/~afilreis/88/kerouac-spontaneous.html.*

AUSTEN

1. Jane Austen, *Emma* (London: John Murray, 1815; Chenango Forks, NY: Wild Jot Press, 2009), 275. Page reference is to the Wild Jot Press edition.

2. Jane Austen, *Sense and Sensibility* (Whitehall, London: Thomas Egerton, Military Library, 1811; New York: E.P. Dutton, 1922), 3, 24, 25, 43. Page references are to the E.P. Dutton edition.

DOYLE

1. Sir Arthur Conan Doyle, *A Study in Scarlet* (London: Ward Lock & Co., 1887; Filiquarian, 2007), 171. Page reference is to the Filiquarian edition.

2. Sir Arthur Conan Doyle, "A Scandal in Bohemia," *The Strand Magazine*, July 1891.

JOYCE

1. Richard Ellman, *James Joyce*, 2nd ed. (New York: Oxford University Press, 1983), 505.

2. James Joyce, *Ulysses* (Paris: Sylvia Beach, 1922), 535. Page reference is to the Kindle edition.

3. James Joyce, *Finnegans Wake* (London: Faber and Faber, 1939; Oxford: Oxford University Press, 2012), 491. Page reference is to the Oxford University Press edition.

SALINGER

1. J.D. Salinger, *The Catcher in the Rye* (New York: Little, Brown and Company, 1951), 275.

TUPAC

1. Connie Bruck, "The Takedown of Tupac," *New Yorker*, July 7, 1997, *http://www.newyorker.com/archive/1997/07/07/1997_07_07_046_TNY_CARDS_000378550.*

2. Tupac Shakur, "Violent," *2Pacalypse Now*, Interscope Records, 1991.

3. Bruck, "The Takedown of Tupac."

4. Cheo Coker, review of *Me Against the World*, by Tupac Shakur, *Rolling Stone*, February 2, 1998, *http://www.rollingstone.com/music/albumreviews/me-against-the-world-19980202.*

5. Tupac Shakur, "So Many Tears," *Me Against the World*, Interscope Records, 1995.

WOOLF

1. Virginia Woolf, *To the Lighthouse* (London: Hogarth Press, 1927; New York: Harcourt Brace Jovanovich, 1989), 127. Page reference is to the Harcourt edition.

2. Virginia Woolf, *Passionate Apprentice: The Early Journals, 1897–1909*, ed. Mitchell A. Leaska (New York: Mariner Books, 1992), xxv.

3. Virginia Woolf, *Mrs. Dalloway* (London: Hogarth Press, 1925; New York: Mariner Books, 1990), 30. Page reference is to the Mariner Books edition.

CHAUCER

1. A basic glossary of Middle English can be found at *http://pages.towson.edu/duncan/glossary.html.*

2. Geoffrey Chaucer, "General Prologue," *The Canterbury Tales*.

3. Geoffrey Chaucer, "General Prologue," *The Canterbury Tales*, trans. Ronald L. Ecker and Eugene J. Crook (Palatka, FL: Hodge & Braddock, 1993).

NABOKOV

1. Vladimir Nabokov, *Speak, Memory* (London: Victor Gollancz Ltd, 1951; New York: Vintage Books, 1989), 59. Page reference is to the Vintage Books edition.

2. Vladimir Nabokov, *Lectures on Literature*, ed. Fredson Bowers (New York: Harvest, 1980; New York: Mariner Books, 2002), 374. Page reference is to the Mariner Books edition.

3. Vladimir Nabokov, *Pnin* (London: Heinemann, 1957; New York: Vintage Books, 1989), 38. Page reference is to the Vintage Books edition.

4. Conrad Brenner, "Nabokov: The Art of the Perverse," *New Republic*, June 23, 1958, *http://www.newrepublic.com/article/books-and-arts/nabokov-the-art-the-perverse*.

BORGES

1. "Jorge Luis Borges, The Art of Fiction No. 39," interview by Ronald Christ, *Paris Review*, no. 40, Winter–Spring 1967, *http://www.theparisreview.org/interviews/4331/the-art-of-fiction-no-39-jorge-luis-borges*.

2. Ibid.

3. Jorge Luis Borges, prologue to *Ficciones*, trans. Anthony Bonner et al. (New York: Grove Press, 1962; paperback edition, 1994), 15. Page reference is to the paperback edition.

4. Jorge Luis Borges, "The Library of Babel" in *Ficciones*, trans. Andrew Kerrigan (New York: Grove Press, 1962; paperback edition, 1994), 82. Page reference is to the paperback edition.

CARROLL

1. Lewis Carroll, *Alice's Adventures in Wonderland* (London: Macmillan, 1865; New York: Dover Publications, Inc., 1993), 46. Page reference is to the Dover edition.

ADAMS

1. Douglas Adams, *The Hitchhiker's Guide to the Galaxy* (London: Pan Books, 1979; New York: Harmony Books, 1989), 156. Page reference is to the Harmony Books edition.

2. Douglas Adams, interview by Gregg Pearlman, March 27, 1987, *http://scifi.stackexchange.com/questions/4211/what-were-some-of-douglas-adamss-hhggs-influences/60015#60015*.

3. Douglas Adams, *The Salmon of Doubt: Hitchhiking the Galaxy One Last Time* (London: William Heinemann Ltd., and New York: Pocket Books, 2002; New York: Ballantine Books, 2003), xxv. Page reference is to the Ballantine Books edition.

DICKENS

1. After "She was dead. Dear, gentle, patient, noble Nell was dead." Charles Dickens, *The Old Curiosity Shop* (London: Chapman & Hall, 1841; London: Wordsworth Editions Ltd., 1998), 529. Page reference is to the Wordsworth edition.

2. After "Oh, Ned, Ned, Ned, what a happy day this is for you and me!" (Charles Cheeryble to his brother Edwin). Charles Dickens, *Nicholas Nickleby* (London: Chapman & Hall, 1839; reprinted 1866), 412. Page reference is to the 1866 edition.

WALLACE

1. Tim Adams, "Karen Green: 'David Foster Wallace's Suicide Turned Him into a "Celebrity Writer Dude,"' Which Would Have Made Him Wince," *Observer*, April 9, 2011, *http://www.theguardian.com/books/2011/apr/10/karen-green-david-foster-wallace-interview*.

2. David Foster Wallace, "POP QUIZ 6(A)," *Brief Interviews with Hideous Men* (New York: Little, Brown and Company, 1999), 142. Page reference is to the paperback edition.

3. David Foster Wallace, *Infinite Jest* (New York: Little, Brown and Company, 1996), 8. Page reference is to the paperback edition.

4. David Foster Wallace, *Everything and More, A Compact History of Infinity* (New York: W.W. Norton and Company, 2003).

5. David Foster Wallace, interview by Michael Silverblatt, *Bookworm*, KCRW, April 11, 1996, *http://www.kcrw.com/news-culture/shows/bookworm/david-foster-wallace-3*.

PLATH

1. Sylvia Plath, letter to Warren Plath (April 23, 1956), *Letters Home: Correspondence 1950–1963*, ed. Aurelia Plath (New York: Harper & Row, 1975).

2. Sylvia Plath and Ted Hughes, "Two of a Kind: Poets in Partnership," interview by Owen Leeming, BBC, January 18, 1961 (*http://www.brainpickings.org/index.php/2013/07/16/sylvia-plath-ted-hughes-bbc-interview-1961/*).

3. Sylvia Plath, "Lady Lazarus," *Ariel* (London: Faber and Faber, 1965).

4. Sylvia Plath, *The Unabridged Journals of Sylvia Plath*, ed. Karen V. Kukil (St. Louis, MO: San Val, 2000; New York: Anchor Books, 2000), 31. Page reference is to the Anchor edition.

CALVINO

1. Italo Calvino, *Letters 1941–1985*, ed. Michael Wood, trans. Martin McLaughlin (Princeton, NJ: Princeton University Press, 2013), 42.

2. Italo Calvino, from the introduction to *Our Ancestors*, trans. Archibald Colquhoun (1962).

ROWLING

1. Published as *Harry Potter and the Sorcerer's Stone* in the United States.

ROY

1. Arundhati Roy, *The God of Small Things* (New York: India Ink/Harper Collins, 1997; New York: Random House, 2008), 3. Page reference is to the Random House edition.

2. Ibid., 13.

3. Ibid., 80.

4. Siddhartha Deb, "Arundhati Roy, the Not-So-Reluctant Renegade," *New York Times Magazine*, March 5, 2014, *http://www.nytimes.com/2014/03/09/magazine/arundhati-roy-the-not-so-reluctant-renegade.html*.

5. Angus Croll, "JavaScript and Russian Dolls," *JavaScript, JavaScript* (blog), April 27, 2010, *http://javascriptweblog.wordpress.com/2010/04/27/the-russian-doll-principle-re-writing%C2%A0functions%C2%A0at%C2%A0runtime/*.

KAFKA

1. Max Brod, *Franz Kafka, a Biography*, trans. G. Humphreys Roberts and Richard Winston (New York: De Capo Press, 1995), 24.

2. Ibid., 178.

3. Franz Kafka, *The Metamorphosis, A Hunger Artist, In the Penal Colony, and Other Stories*, trans. Ian Johnston (Arlington, VA: Richer Resources Publications, 2009), 99-100.

About The Author

Originally from the UK, Angus now works for Twitter's UI framework team in San Francisco and is the co-author and principal maintainer of Twitter's open source Flight framework. He's obsessed with JavaScript and literature in equal measure and is a passionate advocate for the greater involvement of artists and creative thinkers in software. Angus is a frequent speaker at conferences worldwide. He can be reached on Twitter at @angustweets.